GOING UP THE HOLY MOUNTAIN

Gary Hastings

Going Up The Holy Mountain
A Spiritual Guidebook

the columba press

First published in 2015 by

the columba press

55A Spruce Avenue,
Stillorgan Industrial Park,
Blackrock, Co. Dublin

Cover design and illustrations by Helene Pertl / The Columba Press
Cover photography by Eamonn McCarthy
Front image: Old School House, Croagh Patrick, Co. Mayo
Back image: Croagh Patrick

Origination by The Columba Press
Printed by ScandBook, Sweden

ISBN 978 1 78218 179 8

GOD SAID TO ALL THE HOLY
PEOPLE OF IRELAND, OF THE PAST,
THE PRESENT AND THE FUTURE:
'HOLY ONES, CLIMB TO THE TOP OF
THE MOUNTAIN THAT RISES ABOVE
AND IS HIGHER THAN ALL THE
MOUNTAINS OF THE SUN'S WEST,
THAT THE PEOPLE OF IRELAND
MAY BE BLESSED, THAT PATRICK
MAY SEE THE FRUITS OF HIS
LABOURS.

BISHOP TIRECHÁN'S ACCOUNT OF
ST PATRICK'S JOURNEY
ST PATRICK'S WORLD, 169

IN DAYS TO COME THE MOUNTAIN OF THE LORD'S HOUSE
SHALL BE ESTABLISHED AS THE HIGHEST OF THE MOUNTAINS,
AND SHALL BE RAISED ABOVE THE HILLS;
ALL THE NATIONS SHALL STREAM TO IT.
MANY PEOPLES SHALL COME AND SAY,
'COME, LET US GO UP TO THE MOUNTAIN OF THE LORD,
TO THE HOUSE OF THE GOD OF JACOB;
THAT HE MAY TEACH US HIS WAYS
AND THAT WE MAY WALK IN HIS PATHS.'
FOR OUT OF ZION SHALL GO FORTH INSTRUCTION,
AND THE WORD OF THE LORD FROM JERUSALEM.
HE SHALL JUDGE BETWEEN THE NATIONS,
AND SHALL ARBITRATE FOR MANY PEOPLES;
THEY SHALL BEAT THEIR SWORDS INTO PLOUGHSHARES,
AND THEIR SPEARS INTO PRUNING-HOOKS;
NATION SHALL NOT LIFT UP SWORD AGAINST NATION,
NEITHER SHALL THEY LEARN WAR ANY MORE.

ISAIAH 2:1–5

Watching the Mountain

24 December
It wears a dark face.
Hard to imagine anyone
Going up or down.

25 December
Just look. Add nothing.
For nothing is added. Let
It find our wonder.

26 December
Winds scale past gale force.
The whole world seems to break.
The mountain stands still.

27 December
In the night snow fell.
Hard to find it now. Snow clouds.
Snow earth. Snow mountain.

28 December
Watch long enough and
Mists and clouds as they move show
What cannot be seen.

29 December
Just the peak. A fin
Cutting the surface of cloud.
Fear of the unknown.

30 December
At dawn the slow light
Moves down the slopes.
A pilgrim
Known only when known.

31 December
Almost a full moon
Silhouettes the hill. They play
Some air beyond me.

Patrick O'Brien, 2002

Foreword

It's always a testing question: 'Which books would you bring with you to a desert island, presuming you have the Bible and the Complete Shakespeare?' Thomas Merton's *Conjectures of a Guilty Bystander* would always be my first choice. In it a great Christian spirit dialogues with all the great questions of our age and does so open to the spirit of other Christian churches, to the riches of other religions and to the quest revealed in modern writers and thinkers. 'For myself,' he writes, 'I am more and more convinced that my job is to clarify something of the tradition that lives in me, and in which I live: the tradition of wisdom and spirit that is found not only in Western Christendom but in Orthodoxy, and also, at least analogously, in Asia and in Islam.' At different times I may have other books in mind for that desert island, depending on mood and new interests or sudden discovery. I always felt that the chosen books should include something deep and inspirational on prayer, meditation, contemplation. The desert island at its best or worst might invite the good or evil spirits. But it is difficult to find a work on prayer which is fresh, open to the many roads towards God. In this work of Gary Hastings we may all have found an *anam chara* for that journey.

It is written in the voice of a friend, minds and spirits converse. I imagine it as spoken in a quiet corner of a country pub where friends are speaking their lives and in the background musicians are playing tin whistles, fiddles, flutes. And the music enters the conversation and sometimes the voice when it speaks of prayer, or prays, becomes music itself. Gary speaks out of the depths of his own tradition in the Church of Ireland. So many of its great figures shared a love of St Patrick, of the *Book of Kells*, of the Irish language itself as bearers of the wisdom of God in everything that is: in art and music, in the landscape, in the poetry of hermits on islands, in wind and rain and love. And in this book, as indeed in his life as servant of God, he finds the spirit of God at work in other traditions and religions. Only those immersed in their own wonders and truths are in a freedom to encounter the truth dancing elsewhere. At a time of fracture and breakage, of loss of faith in large structures, when the word 'religion' almost demands the qualification 'post' it is necessary to rediscover the roots of our spirits which can only grow when drenched with the rain/reign of God.

It is fitting that this work sets itself in the mountainscape of Croagh Patrick. St Patrick has been this past century rediscovered as one of the great mystical saints whose words sing with the choir of the Trinity of God's love, as the spirit of a community which knows itself only in communion also with the world of nature, as a speaker of freedom for the slaves of the world. In this book we find the pilgrim to Patrick's mountain at one with all who seek the sacred on different mountains, by other seas. Or rather all who allow themselves to be found by the sacred which is everywhere and prays all into unity, compassion, mercy.

One of the many beauties of this book is its tone of voice. In introducing many forms of prayer and contemplation Gary has the grace of a good teacher. You feel the words are tested and tried and you are cared for. You are accompanied on the journey by one who knows the direction and the dangerous turns. Beyond that, in some of the later chapters, a book about prayer becomes a book of prayer. Some of the riches of the

Christian traditions – the Stations of the Cross in the new scriptural version, and the Stations of the Resurrection – are given a voice which speaks out of our time and place. There are also profound meditations on aspects of nature – air, fire, water, stone, soil, light, plants, animals – which in their clarity seem to me to offer a place where the great traditions of East and West meet and offer a way into our common future.

I wrote earlier that this book has the wonder of a conversation in a room where a *seisiún* is also happening. But Gary is not just one of the voices in the conversation. He is also playing the flute, as indeed he does, and this book has the woodwind grace of light and the passion of its breath and fire.

Listen to his words. Hear the music. Join the conversation. Dance to the music.

Patrick O'Brien

Acknowledgements

My thanks to all who helped in any way in the making of this book, intentionally or unintentionally, aware or unaware of their assistance. So much from my reading, so much learned in conversation with friends. Ba mhaith liom go speiseálta mo bhuíochas a ghabháil le mo bhean chéile fhadfhulangach Caitríona, agus lenár mbeirt pháiste, Conn and Caitlín, who together with Rev. Stephen Fielding and Canon Maureen Ryan suffered far beyond the call of duty through reading the first versions of the text, and many thanks to them for their (gentle) comments and advice. Sincere thanks too to Fr Pat O'Brien for friendship over the years. A deep well of wisdom. I don't say that about many. Mention must be made of Chris Smith, who seeded this idea in my head some years ago, and behold it grew! My thanks to the Bishop of Tuam, Killala and Achonry, the Right Reverend Patrick Rooke for allowing me to take the sabbatical during which I wrote this text (may he live forever!), Mr Harry Hughes of Westport for his great generosity in sharing his knowledge and resources with me, and all in Columba Press.

Contents

Locations of Cross Slabs Illustrated
CHAPTER ONE Caher Island, Co. Mayo
CHAPTER TWO Gallarus, Co. Kerry
CHAPTER THREE Kilvickadownig, Co. Kerry
CHAPTER FOUR Ballyvourney, Co. Cork
CHAPTER FIVE Caher Island, Co. Mayo
CHAPTER SIX Glencolmcille, Co. Donegal
CHAPTER SEVEN Killegar, Co. Wicklow
CHAPTER EIGHT Kilnasaggart, Co. Armagh

FAQ

What's this book about?

What does it all mean?

What does 'holy' or 'sacred' mean?

How do I go up a mountain in a spiritual way?

Why do mountains work?

What has all this got to do with my own faith or church or denomination?

So, can I do this if I'm not a Catholic? And what if I'm not a Christian?

What does the Bible say about all this?

How do I get in touch with God?

Is God at the top of the mountain?

Will this help me? Will it make a difference?

What does 'spirituality' mean?

What's the difference between spirituality and religion?

What is this neutral religious technology you keep on about?

What's this book about?

This book is about the real mountain of rock and scree, Cruach Phádraig, Croagh Patrick, or the Reek, in Co. Mayo in the west of Ireland. A mountain with a long pre-Christian and Christian pilgrimage tradition, going back perhaps three thousand years. This book discusses the origins of the pilgrimage, how it is traditionally done, and suggests other ways you might use the mountain as a spiritual resource. But the book can be about a number of other mountains as well.

It can be about any mountain, or hill, or special place we use to do a pilgrimage to, or on. Pick your spot, and the techniques described in this book will help you make spiritual use of that place, or the pilgrimage journey on which you are travelling. Put one foot in front of the other in a spiritual way, and see where it takes you!

It can be about the mountain which stands for our lives, our growing up and maturing, growing old and dying, and how we pass through that process and how far we get during it. The spiritual techniques described here will be of use to us all through our lives, and help us to understand ourselves at a deeper level.

It can be about the mountain which is our spiritual life, growing in spiritual maturity and insight, wisdom and clarity, as we progress towards God. The methods of prayer and meditation given here are ways of approaching and talking to God, learning about God, and, what's more important, establishing and growing a relationship with God. Inviting God into our lives, and making that living presence part of how we think and see the world.

What does it all mean?
This 'climbing mountains in a spiritual way' lark? It means you're a human being. Humans have always done this kind of thing, and continue to do it. Our culture and thinking may have changed from our ancestors' way of seeing and understanding the world, but our heads are still wired to work the same way as theirs. This ritual/religion/spirituality stuff rings our bells and presses our buttons. It still works for people. There are some things we have to remember though:

It's not magic. Really mind-blowing, cool, awesome, amazing things are unlikely to happen, but you may at least begin to achieve a greater calm and connectedness, a deeper understanding of who you are, what your life is about, and what your place might be in this vast universe.

It's not easy. It takes time to learn to do these things, it takes practice and effort and application. It's not an instant fix, it's a skill you acquire with a bit of time and the right way of going about things.

So what it means very much depends on yourself. The experience of climbing the mountain takes on whatever meaning you choose to give it. Tradition, still strong today, gives us some pointers, but it's how your mind and heart are attuned while you do it that gives it any worth. Anyone can ascend this mountain, any mountain, and make it something with more meaning or depth than just a walk. It takes a little thought and preparation, perhaps in the form of sustained awareness as we go up and down the mountain. Or perhaps saying prayers, the traditional ones, if they make sense and resonate with us, or words from this book, or our own prayers. That way we may enter into the tradition of millennia surrounding this mountain. Doing what is a very human thing.

We can use the mountain, the walk, the experience as an aid to take us further, deeper and higher than our feet can ordinarily take us.

What does 'holy' or 'sacred' mean?
The easiest way to explain it is 'special'. Sacred or holy things may look ordinary, just a mountain or a table or a building, but they are 'consecrated' – set aside, reserved for doing special things. For religious purposes. It doesn't mean they have some special power in themselves; it means that they are symbols of something else. They are no longer ordinary, they no longer mean ordinary things. They mean something beyond themselves.

On the Reek, long history, tradition and custom come together to make *this* place, *this* mountain, special and set aside for spiritual purposes, not just the ordinary things of life.

The word 'holy' in English comes from the same origin as 'wholly', meaning complete, and is also related to the word 'health'. That is an important thing to keep in mind. In ourselves, we are not complete. On our own we lack much. We exist only as the result of many things and many people coming together, coming before us. Events and chances and coincidences. We exist only as the result of the community of people around us, making food available, heat, light and company. On our own, our existence would be a miserable one.

Finally and most importantly, we are only whole, only holy, only wholly ourselves when we take our spiritual side into account, and allow God into our life. That is an important ingredient of our true health, physical, mental and spiritual. Sacred, holy places are where we come together to do that, to remember that, and to be reminded of it. In that the holiness of the mountain resides.

How do I go up a mountain in a spiritual way?
You just walk up it, to be honest. This book is intended to help you 'be spiritual' as you go up the mountain. There are ways to pray or meditate or just be present as you go up that will change your experience from just a walk, to something deeper and more fulfilling at many levels.

To go up the mountain in a spiritual way is to use prayer, silent meditation and ritual to keep our minds on our intention, constantly bringing our focus back again and again to what we are doing. It's useful to stop every so often, perhaps for prayers, or perhaps we can just take time to be where we are. Here and now. Something we humans are not very good at. We're inclined to always be somewhere else in our thinking and planning and remembering.

Your intention may just be a simple one, taking time out of your ordinary life to be on your own. Time to pray, time to be silent, or to just 'be'. Many of us, strangely, have never actually got to know ourselves, never spent enough time with ourselves to find out who we really are. This in itself is a very spiritual thing to do. Without a bit of concentration, though, and some kind of structure and discipline, we can spend the day just mentally drivelling to ourselves as usual, and have a nice day out. To be spiritual about it, we have to take a different angle. That's what this book is for. (You might still have a nice day out!)

Why do mountains work?
They're not the same as everywhere else. So they make us feel different when we're on them. Different environments – city streets, forests, grassy fields, the seashore – bring different things out in us. We can use this to help us pray, meditate and think in new ways.

Climb a mountain and the effect is uplifting. Or at least perhaps after you have stopped throwing up, and the double vision fades, and your pulse comes back down to two figures. Oh, and the mist lifts, or if you don't have to hold on to the ground to stop being blown away. Then, it's undeniably uplifting, stirring. It's what makes people climb mountains, one after another. It's what makes them go up Everest, or trudge up some lump of heathery bog which sticks its head up out of the mire. The top of a mountain has a different feel, has an effect on us. And that effect can be used spiritually. That's what we are about here.

Of course you don't have to use a mountain. Anywhere quiet and secluded that gives you 'time out' is suitable. Many places in the world were considered sacred in the past: temples and monasteries and churches, but before that, caves and glens, rocks and mountains, springs and wells all had connections for people with spiritual things. You could use one of those if there was one handy. It doesn't have to be 'your' church or denomination or even religion. But please be careful not to cause offence in any way in places you are not accustomed to be. Be sensitive, non-judgemental and understanding of what other people are doing.

You can create your own sacred space. A corner of a room, or even of a garden, where you can make yourself comfortable, and where you won't be disturbed, with perhaps a seat, some flowers, a candle, incense. Pictures of people you love, a religious picture or object that has a meaning for you. A copy of the Bible, or another book that has great meaning for you. Not too much clutter, but something to bring meaning to the place. To mark it as special.

Having said all that, none of this is necessary or obligatory. You can meditate or pray on a bus, a train, or in a crowded, noisy place – it just takes more practice! But silence, withdrawal, and space helps, and also mental associations connected with the sacred places which are special for you and mean something for you.

What has all this got to do with my own faith or church or denomination?
Nothing and everything. Most faiths have pilgrimage as part of their tradition. All faiths have prayer. Christian churches differ a lot on what they do and what they don't do, and sometimes base their preferences on not doing what some other church is doing. Which doesn't make much sense, really, and is surely not a good reason for doing or not doing anything, but people are like that!

Pilgrimage is simply a journey made for spiritual reasons, a journey accompanied by prayer and made in a prayerful way, and in this case the pilgrimage involves ascending a mountain. It's an aid to prayer, an assistance in our spiritual life. This is a form of neutral spiritual technology. A way of being spiritual and prayerful that can be used by someone of any faith or church or persuasion. Pilgrimage is simply a way of affording time for prayer and reflection, taking time out from ordinary life to be with God, assisted by movement and travel. Kinetic religion, if you like. The mountain, the climbing, the air and wind and rain and rocks can all give a new background and a fresh atmosphere to our prayer life.

So, can I do this if I'm not a Catholic? And what if I'm not a Christian?
Yes. And yes again. For a start, this is a mountain, for heaven's sake, not a private church or chapel. It is owned in common by a number of farmers, it has been used for generations before the Reformation happened, and for generations before Christianity happened.

You are welcome here, whoever you are, and from whatever denomination or faith you come, whatever country, class, race or gender you belong to. Here we are all one under the sky, loved by God, and required to respond to his love. This is a good place to do that in. No more, no less.

A mountain is a bit of neutral religious technology that is truly international, ecumenical and interfaith. While Cruach Phádraig has traditional Christian significance in Ireland, there is no reason why you might not join in using it respectfully for spiritual purposes if you are of another faith. There need be no offence taken in one person praying beside another if we accept each other in love.

If you are of no faith at all, you may derive great advantage from the peace, relaxation, and physical and mental benefits just spending time in a beautiful place can bring you. Meditation can be approached purely from a psychological angle, and can bring great well-being and reward when practised regularly.

Please respect the religious practices of others, even if you do not share or believe in them yourself. Try to understand what is happening, with patience and kindness, and see the deeper underlying spirituality and humanity within. That way we can begin to disentangle and understand our own inherited and acquired opinions and predispositions.

Whatever your faith or opinions, please treat this mountain with respect. You are welcome to use the mountain for recreation, of course, but please try not to disturb those who are using it for spiritual purposes. Take home your litter, and remember it is not a public park, or just another amenity.

This is not just a mountain. Nowhere is 'just' what it seems to be.

What does the Bible say about all this?

Mountains in the Bible are places of meaning. We are told that Jesus went up mountains to pray and teach on many occasions in the gospels. Christ may have used such places as sources of inspiration and peace, suitable for the practice of his spirituality. His most famous sermon was supposed to have been given on a mountain (Matthew 5–7); the Ascension, the Feeding Miracles and the Transfiguration all take place on mountains. The last verses of Matthew, after the Resurrection, take place on 'the mountain to which Jesus had directed them', where he commissions the disciples, and tells them he would be with them to the end of the age.

As in the gospels, mountains in the Old Testament have a symbolic presence. Sinai or Horeb, for instance, where we're told Moses received the Commandments, spending forty days and nights in the presence of God; the 'Mountain of God', where Moses saw the burning bush. The idea of a Holy Mountain comes up again and again in the Psalms and the Prophets.

A mountain, as it points to the heavens, is a strong, clear signal and symbol, a holy place and spiritual resource in many cultures and faiths. It can still be an instrument for us to use in our spirituality and worship today.

How do I get in touch with God?

You pray. Prayer means contacting, being with, talking to God. It can be a conversation, a request, for ourselves or someone else. It may be thanks, or complaint, it may express love or anger or hurt. It may not involve words – silent meditation, or it may be a series of meaningful actions, usually called ritual. Walking up the mountain can count, if you do it in the right frame of mind. Even just breathing, being, looking around you, hearing the wind, the birds, other people, distant cars and tractors and diggers. Any of these things, if you do them on purpose, with your mind pointing the right way, can be forms of prayer.

This book can help you start. See the sections on prayer or meditation for example. (Chapters Six and Seven. You don't need to wrap your legs around your neck!) Or look at the Stations further on in the book. These are for reading in a prayerful way; silently or aloud; slowly and attentively. They might help a bit.

One thing to remember is that God is there/here and aware of you. Always, everywhere. All you have to do is turn towards God. If you don't know what to say, don't say anything. Just be there. Be aware of the love, acceptance and compassion that is there for you. You don't have to do anything, just open up to it. Relax into it. Trust it.

You may not hear or see or feel anything. That's ok. Neither do most people most of the time. You have to relax and have trust. It takes time, and a different way of thinking.

So how do you pray? Talk to God. Start yesterday. Read books about it. Ask stupid questions and make the life of your local cleric worthwhile!

Is God at the top of the mountain?

Yes. He's also at the bottom, half way up, and back home wherever you came from. The mountain is just a way of thinking. A tool to help us get nearer God. We are always close to God, but we forget, we blank it out. The mountain is a way to help us to remember. Perhaps it helps to think that we are closer to God at the top of the mountain, having climbed up so far. Perhaps people centuries ago thought that way. But having been up, we can bring God back down with us into our ordinary lives, and that way find out that they aren't so ordinary after all.

Will this help me? Will it make a difference?
Yes, and yes. But it isn't magic or instant. It takes time, and you have to learn to do it, and that's not easy. Simple, but not easy. If you wish to learn about spirituality, that takes time and effort and work. What is there that doesn't? If you wish to progress in your faith, learn and grow in it, that takes time and effort as well. We have to put the effort in, and take the time to do it, and then things in our lives can change.

Having said all that, you may be at a place in your life where a very small thing can bring about great change. You may be under emotional pressure or stress; you may be thinking and praying about something; you may have suffered something – a bereavement, an illness, a loss, a great hurt – and just doing something about it can bring great relief. People did practices like this in the past because they derived something from it.

What does 'spirituality' mean?
I'm using the word in this book to convey the idea of the search for meaning. The meaning of something is its inherent, central truth. It's not easy to put your finger on it, and lots of people will see it in varying ways, depending on who they are and what their culture is. Our perception of truth can change from moment to moment. In spiritual terms, you might say that you have to see with the eyes of your heart, not your head. You have to see and think differently from usual.

Words are very crude tools for discussing things like spirituality, as you will notice if you have read down this far! Words point towards the thing they indicate, but, like signposts in real life, they don't go all the way to the place they're pointing to. They don't go far or deep enough beyond the level of simply labelling. Just knowing and using the words isn't the same as experiencing the reality behind them.

Spirituality tends to be a bit soft and bendy and blurred. This is good because it allows creativity and flexibility and breadth. This is bad because it allows some people to talk rubbish and lead you (and themselves) astray. Be aware of this.

What's the difference between spirituality and religion?
Spirituality, as I say above, means no more than the search for meaning in life. Everyone is interested in that to some extent. You may or may not get very far. It's hard to keep up with such a search in our world when there's so much to distract you from it, or so many conflicting suggestions for ways of doing it. Spirituality implies a personal and private thing, whereas a religion is something a group of people are doing publicly in an organised way. All religions involve spirituality, but not necessarily vice versa. Religion tends to have a negative press, but in fact most of the older forms of faith have been used for thousands of years by millions of people, and not all of them were 'following blindly'. Tradition has polished and honed the older faiths to a fine edge. They reflect reality in that they have soft bits and hard bits, easy bits and difficult bits and they have developed checks and balances along the way. Just because people lived long ago doesn't mean they were stupid! You could say that a religion is a ready-made spiritual path or device which we use together with other people to help us grow a relationship with God. The religion itself isn't the point, it's where it takes us.

I'm a Christian, and not an expert on other faiths, but Christianity works for me. Your own personal and cultural background will obviously influence you in any choice of faith or variety of Christianity, but you will have the security in knowing that others have gone this way before you and left a track for you to follow. The first name for Christianity was 'The Way', after all. You are also allowed (and recommended) to bring your common sense and reason with you. You don't have to leave it outside the door if you come in. Trust is involved, which is what 'faith' basically means, but you're still allowed to think!

What is this neutral religious technology you keep on about?
In all the faiths, all the religions, all the cults and spiritual practices of humanity, certain things come up again and again. These are the techniques that humans use when they are being religious and spiritual. New faiths, or new and revised versions of old faiths don't stray much from the usual menu. They include, amongst others: prayer, sacrifice, pilgrimage, meditation, communal meals and rituals, the use of bells and prayer beads and robes and incense, temples and churches, priests and monks and nuns, fasting and feasting, sacred texts and books, dancing and music, ritual objects, and the use of symbolism: water, fire, food, sound, wine, oil, bread, relics; the idea of saints and holiness. We may have many names for them, different reasons for them, but the technologies are much the same and the menu is quite limited.

The Reek, a mountain, is just another religious device; pilgrimage is a religious technique, so is meditation and prayer. All are permitted to Christians and those of other faiths. It is how we use them, what we mean by them, and what we intend by them, that separates faiths or denominations.

Mountain Safety
Please note, that going up mountains entirely on your own is not a good idea. These are not safe places. Please take adequate safety precautions. Deaths occur on the Reek, or on any mountain from one cause or another. Be sensible. Better to go with other people. It is a good idea to tell someone where you're going, what route you're taking and what time you

expect to be back. Expect bad weather, and take clothing suitable for it. Wear the right footwear for a mountain. Take first-aid gear. Don't expect your mobile phone to work up there. Take food and water with you.

All this is just common sense.

That's on a real mountain. On the mountain that is your spiritual life, you also need to take care. It's not easy, you can be led astray and get lost. Keep your common sense with you at all times. You may become discouraged, and can have doubts. Expect some subsidence, trip hazards and mental weather problems. Expect light and growth and insights as well. Ask advice, other people have gone this way before. There is help available, and support and company for the journey.

All this is just common sense.

CHAPTER TWO

Setting Out

Cruach Phádraig is a special place sacred for millennia. It is webbed and wrapped by a network of ancient monuments and associations; standing stones, cross-slabs, stone alignments, abbeys, wells, Christian and pre-Christian sacred sites, the scar of the pilgrimage path on its side. The very sun itself rolls ritually down its slopes once a year. All these things are markers to show that this place is considered special.

We need special places. Humans have created them all through history. Or have used what nature presented them with. This is a guidebook for use in any special place, not just the one on the cover. It is a collection of meditations, of instructions on how to behave, how to think, how to pray and be reverend and open to the possibilities of a special place. It's not meant as a total departure from what has gone before, but it provides a new spin on older practices, and an entry-level introduction for those who are outside, but might like to come in.

Some places are called 'holy' by convention. That specialness may simply be because of geography, or because someone once had an experience there, and tradition seeks to remember or share in the experience afterwards. We can also make places special for ourselves. By our own personal associations, by intention and conscious act we can make the ordinary special, or more exactly, appreciate the special in the ordinary.

Our day-to-day awareness of reality is very limited in one way. We live in a time where intense sensory stimulation can be ours for the asking at any hour of the day or night. Where once music and art, story and song, and even food and drink were luxuries, now we are being sold things, told things, tempted by things, relentlessly and continually. Our mental life is swamped with the input from smartphones, tablets, computers, TV, advertising, internet, video games, news-papers and magazines. Soaps and novels, songs and images. Our mental pathways are rarely free of stimulation in one form or another. For someone from a previous era of our history much of our ordinary everyday life would be like a rowdy, technicolour, explosive, hallucinogenic experience. Thus true reality, which doesn't happen on TV, gets crowded out, drowned out. Real life, just in case you're not sure, is the one with no music in the background and no special effects. It doesn't always feel good, and there may or may not be a happy ending. It can seem pale beside its clever, emotionally stimulating, virtual rivals. Our own mental fantasies, fuelled by all this, carry on singing the soundtracks, continuing the emotional high when outside stimulation is not available. Humans could always dream, as the old stories show us, but they weren't able to live inside a dream, as we almost can.

To return to unadorned, straightforward reality is also to return to the sacred, to God. God is present, always and everywhere. God is the basis of reality. God is truth. These last two deceptively simple phrases, if unpicked, would fill more than one book. But wherever we are, God is. Wherever we are, the sacred is part of our experience. Except we have tuned it out. Instead of listening to the God wavelength, we are tuned into plastic, garish, synthetic stimuli. The God wavelength isn't made up of hymns, prayers, Bible readings and sermons, inspiring messages and requests for donations, thank God! The God wavelength broadcasts silence. It underlies and surrounds and exists within reality. It is the gap between the words, which allows them to make sense. It is the pause between the musical notes, which allows the tune to form. It is the space around and behind our thoughts, that which bears us up and creates us anew every instant. The gap between breaths, heartbeats. But many of us don't hear it, can't see it, and aren't really sure where to start looking. Well, somewhere special is a good place to start. Up a mountain, for example!

Any mountain will do. Consecration means to set something aside for special use. We can do that for ourselves. It can be a mountain, or a garden, or a bus shelter. Even a corner of your mind. Whatever you have, wherever it is, God will be there. God is wherever *you* happen to be, whatever time it is. The place itself is only a tool. In terms of God's presence it is no different from any other place on the planet. But in terms of how humans think and see things, in terms of how our brains work, it can be special. So this book is for your own private mountain, the one most accessible to you. Even if it's just in your eye, your heart, your mind, and your walking, scrambling, climbing days have passed.

The meditations and practices given here are for anyone to do anywhere. Practices is a good way to think of them. We practise something to become better at it, but that isn't the end of the matter. The best professional musicians practise the most and don't ever stop. It's not just how they get where they are, but also how they stay there. Practise is an integral part of *being* a good musician, not only the way to get there. We also say that a doctor has a 'practice'. Being a doctor is what s/he does, that is their practice. So too with prayer and meditation. They are not special things that we do occasionally when the notion takes us or when a need arises in our life. Prayer, meditation, being with God – living in reality– is what we are, are what we do. Not 'should', 'ought', or 'are supposed to do'. Prayer and meditation are ways of being with God, being aware of God, living with God. And if God is that in whom we 'live and move and have our being', that practice must be part of what we are. It is the point of our existence, above and beyond simple survival, eating and drinking and sleeping and staying warm. We don't stop one and do the other, instead we become aware of the one within the other. Practise is what we do to keep our minds in that awareness. To stop practising is to allow our old habits, our old ways of thinking to come back in; to allow the conditioning of previous years to take over again, and drown out the silent voice of God. Our Lord didn't stop praying when he got to a certain stage. His prayer was part of his life, was his life, right up to the very end.

This book, these meditations and suggestions are only a starting place. This book has been written because the Pilgrimage on Reek Sunday now exists in a very different age from the ones that came before. Religion and the prevailing culture are no longer in the same relationship with each other. Increasingly, people are no longer naturally reared in a domestic religious culture, and the idea of prayer, let alone pilgrimage, is becoming a very distant one. The intense faith practices of the generations before us are fading, even amongst those who still profess belief, still attend a church weekly, still say their prayers. Rather than something still worthwhile in itself, with benefits relevant for today, the traditional practices of the Cruach Phádraig pilgrimage, and indeed, even ordinary religious activity, may now seem alien and unintelligible to disaffected generations. At the same time many people still feel a spiritual need, and this book is intended to fill that in some way.

Humans have not changed. We still have, as the modern phrase has it, 'a spiritual side'. Old ways have still a lot to commend them. The generations who came before us left the track of their hand on them, and done aright and in the right frame of mind, they are effective and dependable and safe paths to the divine at the core of our existence. They might need new wheels and a paint job, but they still run!

The Reek is increasingly used as a resource for leisure activities. People walking, running, cycling, sightseers, day-trippers, climbers and hikers and naturalists and photographers. This book is for them. For you. It is a book of instructions and practices to enable you to contact God. It will allow you and empower you to live in a less cluttered reality. It will connect you with peace, fuel hope and inspire faith. If you do it. Only if you do it. Reading the book is not enough, keeping it on a shelf is not enough, owning it is not enough. (Borrowing it is especially not enough. Buy yer own!)

Pilgrimage is an important concept, both in Christianity and in most other faiths. It was seriously undervalued and mostly set aside by the reformed churches, and had become unfashionable even in those churches who still practise it. It has recently become more popular, as travel has become easier, leisure time more available, and fitness more desirable. The Camino, the long tramp from France to Santiago de Compostela is now well known and done for all sorts of reasons as well as the traditional religious ones. Lourdes, Medjugorje, Fatima, and Knock draw large numbers of devotees of a more traditional religious type, though perhaps of older generations. Lough Derg in Donegal has experienced a resurgence in recent years, and of all the pilgrimages, could not be classed as mere entertainment.

The Reek has held its own though. The crowds it attracts on the last Sunday in July are still big. Mostly, they know why they are there, they know what they are supposed to do, and how to do it. But in the wider population, an increasing number of people have no idea of how to go about such a thing, or why to bother. They have fallen out of the container of tradition, and it seems a closed book to them. Their perception of it might be as exclusive, exotic, superstitious, anachronistic and irrelevant. But the perception would be wrong. This is still a useful device for someone to have in his or her spiritual toolkit, in their life. It is above all practical and real. It involves concrete action and movement. It is not shrouded in words and theology; it is something you just do. Intellect, education or station in life are besides the point. And while you do it, because you do it, things can change. You can change; your view of ordinary life, of what is going on, changes and is changed. You leave yourself open to possibility, to the chance of hearing the silence, seeing the meaning.

To go on pilgrimage, to go somewhere on purpose, for a spiritual reason, has a logic to it that resonates with many people. To remove oneself from ordinary life, even for a short while, and go somewhere else, not merely to arrive, but to invest the travel and movement itself with meaning is what pilgrimage is about. It is one of the neutral religious technologies, common to most faiths in the world. People do it, have always done it, because it works, it makes a difference. Spirituality is part of life, part of what we are, and to do a pilgrimage is to experience our life in miniature. We start at A and end up at B. We grow, we develop, we mature, we change. And then there is an end to it all, or perhaps a return, a homecoming. To make sense of this big life journey within a little one, a symbolic one, is the point of pilgrimage; the microcosm reflecting the macrocosm. And it is also time out, physical activity, relaxing, meeting people, having experiences, achieving something.

So to ascend the mountain with a spiritual intention is a pilgrimage. That also includes the time spent getting to the bottom of the mountain and going home again, not just the ascent and descent. To keep the intention constantly in mind, to keep ourselves constantly in the consciousness of God's presence, there are lots of things we can do. What *you* will choose to do, what will work and make sense for you will need not be the same as other people. If you are on your own, one technique is better than another. If you are with a group or a crowd, perhaps you should do at least some things communally, and another approach will suit best.

This book is to suggest what you might try as you do your pilgrimage. Remember that pilgrimage is not just a once-off day out, or longer trip. It is your entire life. Many of the topics and techniques mentioned here can take years to learn and practise and perfect. There is time to do that. But the point of them is to keep us in consciousness of God's presence above all other things. Being 'good' at them is only a secondary consideration.

CHAPTER THREE

What does it Mean?

The massive annual pilgrimage on Cruach Phádraig has deep religious significance for the people taking part. This chapter will explore how that came about, what form it takes today, and what the sense of such a practice is. It has continued through linguistic, cultural and religious shifts over a very long time, 'shedding skins' as it went, if you like. The practices of prayer, meditation and pilgrimage still have resonance and use in the twenty-first century, whoever and wherever we are, and anyone can avail of a mountain, a short trip, a walk, a spare half day, to bring spiritual fulfilment to their lives.

Layers of Meaning

Cruach Phádraig carries ideas, associations and meanings piled up as thick as the rocks and ruins our ancestors left behind them on it. Metaphors and perceptions, stories and traditions. They are there if we wish to use them to illuminate our own thinking, to channel it or broaden it.

The mountain has a number of names: Cruach Phádraig, Croagh Patrick (St Patrick's Stack, or Rick). 'Reek' is a local pronunciation of the word rick. The top of the mountain looks exactly like its agricultural namesake. On first impression the mountain stands alone, looking higher than its 765 metres and is visible from over thirty miles away. Our ancestors, like humans all over the globe when presented with a mountain, came to the opinion it must be a holy place.

As well as geology, there are layers of tradition and concept on the mountain. The layers of meaning on the Reek are not simple and discrete. Older things are reinterpreted in newer times, reused. People look back and see through different eyes. Languages and faiths change. Ideas come and go. All this shows the importance this place had for previous generations. It attracted them, interested them and stimulated them to think and imagine and explore – and pray.

The earliest levels of meaning and use are visible in archaeological remains in the vicinity, going back to Neolithic times indicating that the Reek may be part of a huge ritual landscape. The nearby Boheh Stone, or 'St Patrick's Chair' is one of the most important Neolithic rock art sites in Ireland and Britain. It is covered in 'Cup and Ring' markings and other symbols. In the 1990s, Gerry Bracken, a local scholar, discovered the 'rolling sun' phenomenon connected with it. Standing at Boheh, the sun seems to sit on the top of the mountain and rolls down it as it sets on 18 April (Spring) and 24 August (Harvest), 'dates significant in the sowing and harvest cycles of contemporary civilisations'. 'The spectacle would have resembled a golden disk rolling down one side of a perfect triangle before disappearing into darkness' (Morahan, p. 29).

The Bronze Age stone alignment in Killadangan lines up on one of the shoulders of the Reek, where the sun disappears on the shortest day of the year. Other standing stones in the general area may have been placed to have the summit of the mountain in view. Many of the hut sites high up on the mountain date from this time as well.

Leacht Benain, or Mionnain, a prehistoric burial cairn from this period, is the first station of the pilgrimage trail. Benan was supposedly St Patrick's charioteer. Other cairns, in Reilig Mhuire (Mary's Graveyard), stations where people circum-ambulate and leave stones, may also be of prehistoric date, but their present ritual and religious significance may not have any especially long history. This is a good example of the layers interacting with each other, as the cairns are much older than the story.

Excavations uncovered the foundations of an 'upturned boat oratory', like the one in Gallarus on the Dingle peninsula in Co. Kerry, within a stone rampart encircling the summit, with hut sites surrounding it.

Such remains show the high status of the mountain over a long time. Oral and written legendary associations would tend to affirm this, in addition to parallels with other Irish mountains and connected ecclesiastical and pagan traditions. Most notably Mount Brandon in Kerry, and Slieve Donard in Co. Down, both associated with Crom Dubh, a pagan god, each with a pilgrimage tradition.

Domhnach Crom Dubh (Crom Dubh's Sunday) is one name of the festival which falls at the end of July or beginning of August, marking the beginning of the harvest season. On that day, people ate a meal of the new staple crops of the year. Local communities all over Ireland and in many parts of the British Isles would go up various local high places or to watersides where they traditionally picked bilberries, and for sports and other festivities. A survival of the Celtic festival of Lughnasa, held on the 1 August, this is the source of the pilgrimage on Cruach Phádraig (Máire MacNeill, *The Festival of Lughnasa*).

Lughnasa was one of the four major annual feasts (Imbolg, Bealtaine and Samhain, 1 February, May, and November,

41

respectively). It is a nativity feast in honour of the Celtic god, Lugh, a god of light. In the legend, Lugh wrests from the great god Crom Dubh (Black Bent One) the fruits of the harvest for his followers. Hence the feasting and celebrations. One god is deposed by another.

The Christian legend attached to the mountain is also of one god deposing another; in this case Crom Dubh, representing the pagan religion, is deposed through the agency of Saint Patrick, standing in for Lugh/Christ, in favour of the Christian faith. The oratory on the summit was presumably to securely and definitively nail the door shut after the pagan god had left. Layers, intertwined and adapted to suit a new context.

The Story of St Patrick and the Reek
And Patrick travelled on to Sliab Aigli [Cruach Phádraig] to fast there for forty days and forty nights, following the example of Moses, Elias and Christ. His charioteer died at Muiriscc Aigli [Murrisk, Co. Mayo], that is, on the plain between the sea and Aigle. There Patrick buried his charioteer, Totus Calvus [Totmael], gathered stones together for his cairn, and said, 'So let him be forever; and he will be visited by me at the end of the world.'
And Patrick went up to the summit of Crochán Aigli and stayed there for forty days and forty nights. And he was tormented by birds gathering towards him so that he couldn't see the sky or the sea or the land ...
Because God said to all the holy people of Ireland, of the past, the present and the future: 'Holy ones, climb to the top of the mountain that rises above and is higher than all the mountains of the sun's west, that the people of Ireland may be blessed, that Patrick may see the fruits

of his labours. ... Because the choir of all the saints of
Ireland came to him, to visit their father.'
Bishop Tirechán's Account of St Patrick's Journey
(*Saint Patrick's World*, 169)

Oral sources tell of Patrick's driving a host of demons into
Log na nDeamhan (The Hollow of the Demons). They fled in
the form of a flock of black crows which may also be the basis
of the idea of his expelling the snakes from Ireland.

In medieval times the Reek was a major pilgrimage site in
Ireland. Ballintubber Abbey (1216), where baths and beds were
available for pilgrims, was built on one of the main pilgrimage
routes, Tóchar Phádraig (Patrick's Causeway). It is still
possible to walk the Tóchar, moving through ancient Christian
and pre-Christian sites. (See www.ballintubberabbey.ie for
details.) By the sea at the foot of the Reek is Murrisk Abbey
(1457) and to the west is Kilgeever Abbey (twelfth century or
earlier).

Between the pre-Christian Lughnasa, the imprimatur given
by St Patrick, and medieval custom, the pilgrimage tradition
is affirmed and continued. In the early nineteenth century,
under the influence of continentally trained clergy, the Church
began to take a dim view of some of the customs of the
peasantry at traditional religious occasions which were
perceived as having 'scandalous' activity in connection with
them: drunkenness and faction fighting, and the usual things
which result from intermingling of the genders! Following the
tragic effects of the Great Famine of the 1840s the pilgrimage
seems to go into abeyance. Later in the nineteenth century
there were moves to revive it, but it was not until 1903 that it
was finally officially reinstated. The night-time part of the
pilgrimage was discouraged in the middle of the twentieth
century, for the same reasons of scandal and drunkenness,

though safety was also a primary concern. Until 1971 the Mass at midnight was the main occasion, with further Masses taking place throughout the night. The line of torches going up the Reek in the dark was remarkable to see. Nowadays, official religious proceedings begin at 8 a.m.

The Present Day
The main day is on the last Sunday in July, when between twenty and thirty thousand people ascend the mountain, some barefoot, with sticks and waterproofs, and ambulance and First Aid personnel and helicopters on call. Stands sell all possible necessities and rent out walking sticks to the pilgrims. All races, ages and genders are represented. Evangelical religious groups at the foot of the mountain hand out tracts declaring it a 'vain and empty superstition', other stands sell religious paraphernalia. There are tourists just there for a look around, large numbers of the Travelling community, for which this is a special event, and pilgrims from all over the world, some fully kitted out for all eventualities, and others determined to be martyrs to style and elegance. The Reek has been climbed in high heels before now, surely a more effective mortification than bare feet. Confession is available, and Mass is celebrated in the chapel on the summit. This building dates from 1905, and the clergy go up early to be there ready for the pilgrims ascending, though some punters still go up at night, whatever about the ban on it.

There's more than one way up. From the Murrisk side, where there are car parks and toilets and a pub and cafe with showers, the main pilgrim route is ground into the face of the mountain and visible for miles. From the other side of the mountain the Tóchar arrives after more than twenty miles wending from one significant religious site to another, and you can ascend along the shoulder of the mountain. The shortest route is from the 'back' of the mountain. It takes a couple of hours on average to go up the main route. This annual pilgrimage is a major event in the lives of many people in Ireland; it is a vibrant living tradition that still resonates strongly and is in no danger of dying out.

What does it all mean?
The stories aren't just stories, the traditions weren't just an excuse for a day out, a bit of craic. These tales and customs associated with the mountain meant something to people at a deep level. The standing stones, rock art, abbeys and pilgrimages gave sense to life and living and dying, to the passing year, to history. They pointed to a hidden future, a hidden, spiritual present. They were sources of structure and meaning for people.

We must approach them with respect and reverence, despite the fact that, culturally, our world is very unlike that of those who went before us, and the gap is still widening very quickly. Much of what and how the people of ancient times thought is lost to us. They are more foreign to us than the most exotic tribespeople now inhabiting the world, and we would be most bizarre and fearsome specimens to them! If the early medieval legend of St Patrick is slightly closer to home than Lugh and Crom Dubh, the society the legend sprang from and whose needs it fulfilled is still very foreign to our own.

Knowing what we know today may mean that what made sense to people 500, 1500, or 3000 years ago, or even only 100 years ago, may no longer resonate with us, may no longer make sense. We should also be aware of projecting back what we want to see, rather than admitting that we don't know what was there. What we do have in common with those who preceded us is that we are humans, and we work much the same way as they did, and are physically no different, if a bit healthier and better fed. We like pleasure and dislike pain. We have families and loves and hates. We need shelter and company and warmth and food and sex and sociability. Like all the members of our species. And we want to know what things mean. Humans have always adored meaning in stories and songs, talk and discussion. All art, music and literature, indeed all religion, is about meaning. In none of that do we differ from our ancestors. Always the idea of meaning and truth has changed and grown to fit the people who used it, to make sense of where and who they were. That much we can still do, that much we can still understand.

The worth of the history of the Reek is not in any of the detail, specifically, but rather in the way the neutral spiritual technology is reused over and over, even though the context has changed from pagan to Christian, and then from a native, colloquial 'Celtic' Christian spirituality, to the revised wider international Christian practices and devotions of the last two centuries. Now, even that style seems threadbare and worn out. 'Redecoration' is required for new times, though with respect and consideration of what came before. Change is happening in Christianity in Ireland, whether we wish for it or not. There is an opportunity to widen the scope of the pilgrimage and reinvigorate it for a new time, a new culture. In our society official religion is going into abeyance; almost all Christian denominations are in decline. The children of the seventies, eighties and nineties in Ireland are finding it harder to understand the faith culture of their parents and grandparents, more than any generation before them. This requires a reinterpretation, new words for old ideas, new ways back into old truths.

The spiritual technology the Reek represents: the pilgrimage, the use of a holy place, prayer and meditation, the solitude of the chapels on the summit, old and new, the monastic life, all that is still of use to us today. If we have 'moved on' in one way, in technological achievement, medicine and science, in another we are still as our ancestors were, humans in search of meaning and fulfilment. Still in awe of where we are placed in the universe and in need of help and direction in our small personal lives and relationships. Still in need of structure, advice and wisdom to run our societies.

Spirituality is a human trait. It's a way of thinking that has real benefits for us. Think of it as a meme, or even as a cultural 'app' if you like, but it suits us, rounds us out, fulfils us, helps us. It is a positive, not a negative thing. Humans have been spiritual and religious for thousands and thousands of years, certainly back to our direct Cro-Magnon ancestors. It is part of being human, part of how we relate to each other as individuals, to the community and society in which we live, and to the world and universe we inhabit. It makes sense of things for us, and sense of our part within those things. These faiths were the places where our ancestors stashed their wisdom; how to live, how to get on with other people, how to be an adult individual, a group, a society. How to be part of this world, this universe; how to relate to existence, to growing up, to death. These religions held and enshrined their highest ideals, their most valued thoughts, woven into stories and myths to stick in memory and psychology, to shape and guide.

The older forms of faith common in our society were once passed on through 'cultural osmosis', but that thread has been broken. Our culture no longer works the same way. New devotional forms will be created and designed by those coming behind us to suit the new contexts in which they find themselves. They may not look or sound the same. Those of us who were raised with an older thing may not like them, but they will work for the people and generations who need them. Christianity and other faiths will survive, I believe, but in new forms answering to new needs, new perceptions.

In part this book is meant as a way in to a new thing, looking at older traditions which have been tried and tested, and bringing in fresh alternatives based on them. The religious devotions of our grandparents are definitely no longer 'cool'. It isn't a matter then of resurrecting ancient aboriginal Celtic practices, or quaint medieval customs, or even worse, retreating into modern spit-flecked, antagonistic funda-mentalism, but of understanding the context, the reasons, the techniques behind and beneath them, and realising that these are still efficacious, still true; they still work for humans and we can and should still use them. The neutral spiritual technologies we have been bequeathed function whatever colour they are painted. The window dressing may be changed, but we still need a window into ourselves, a window into the reality we gloss over and conceptualise and keep at arm's length. The reality where God is.

You have the use of the Reek with all its ancient significance, if you wish to avail of it. Or you have your own 'mountain'. Layer that with meaning. See it with new eyes. Your mountain may not have an official, hallowed history, but it has a present, and a presence. It is what it is, and wherever it is, it is special. God is here, reality is present. This in itself is wonderful. We are able to be here too, to exist, live, and not only that, be conscious of living and being. That is a big deal, and we forget.

Let this place be for you a key to let you in to reality, into a special place that can make all places special. We can see from the very top that God is everywhere, and everywhere is in God. Let the mountain take you up into the kingdom, so that you can bring it down with you again, so you can recognise it in your ordinary life, which is not, ever, ordinary.

CHAPTER FOUR

Mountains, Religion and Your Mind

The Reek has its toes in the island-speckled waters of Clew Bay, its head in the clouds and the bogs and hills of Mayo and Connemara around about it. It has slopes of heather and whins, scree and tough wiry sedge, boulders and craggy sharp rocks. Hard winds and soft winds play around it. A long plume of carded cloud flies from its peak. On other days a thick grey mist, neither water nor air, shrouds and hides it. People say it's 'holy'.

This mountain, any mountain, is an in-between place. It isn't the ordinary flat lowland, grassy field or brown bog, nor a dimpled drumlin or a rolling hill. It is neither earth nor sky. It is a hard place and a lonely one, and a place that points to other things beyond. It is a place stripped of grass and tree, down to the bare bones of existence and the hard sharpness of reality. It is a *díseart* – a desert in the air, implying bare rock, baking sun, blasting wind, driving rain, blinding mist and snow and hard ice; but also it is a *díseart* – a secluded retreat, a place apart. The word in Irish can mean both things. It is neither hospitable nor habitable, but you can make use of it. It can show you life as it really is.

49

This mountain, any mountain, is not a temple or a church made of cut, carved and mortared stones, with the aisles, rails and pews, books and clergy we are used to; it is shifting scree and massive rock, the product of Creation, of glacier, wind and weather. There is no absolute, certain footing here; the answers up here are not the parroted simple solutions you don't need to think about, it isn't all laid out for you. Because this is a church turned inside out and upside down. The rules up here came before commandment and revelation, scripture and prophecy. Up here, up the mountain, there is only reality, reality lifted up above the usual ideas and glib definitions. Up here, words become wobbly and ineffectual. The boundlessness of sky, the spread of the planet beneath us, the immensity of where we live and exist and move and have our being is shown to us. Our own smallness, the true scale of things is held up for us to see, if we want to look. That helps us think, helps us see our lives and thoughts in other ways. We can get to see who we are in ourselves from a new angle. Mountains and places like them can help you to do that if you're interested in finding out. Questions like 'Who am I?' and 'What's it all about?' can get answers in these places. But you have to want to find out.

How does it work?
Down below, the tight ropes of culture and custom, inherited opinions and beliefs hold things tightly together in our minds and lives like the *súgáin* on a thatched roof. The very land itself, if you look down on it from the mountain, is closely and tightly defined and divided. The encircling walls and boundaries, gardens and roads, field and bog and forest, the barbed wire of class, denomination, gender, race and faith, are what we use to divide up and sort out our complicated lives.

Up here, at the top of the mountain, above the human scrapes on the surface, only the four elements exist, and ourselves – and something else. The something else is easier to see up here, easier to comprehend.

How do you go about that?
That's the business of meditation and prayer, something well worth having a go at. But people for millennia have known that meditation and prayer work better in some places than others. Some places have the ability to lever off the top of our heads and let the pressure out. They bring a bit of space into our mental processes, shine some light into our skulls, and we get to understand them more clearly, see more clearly.

What is there to see?
One thing we definitely get to see is our own mentality. (Whether we want to or not!) The processes which go to make up how we think and perceive the world and talk to ourselves about it. Most of us only see what our minds let us see, not what's there. We aren't actually aware of what truly exists, we're only aware of what we think exists. But when you do meditation, when you pray in the right way, then you get glimpses of how you think and function mentally, and you begin to be able to tell the difference between that and reality. Then, if you're lucky, you get to see reality itself.

Reality is the place where (what I call) God is. Not up in heaven, not over there or over here or in a church or holy place. Reality is where God is. We keep ourselves insulated from reality by thinking a lot, talking to ourselves, telling ourselves what everything is, who we are, who everybody else is. Some of this may be correct, but much of it is only opinion, thought, impression, assumption. Reality is where the truth is. And it takes a bit of work to find it. That work is spiritual work. Spiritual work will involve your heart and your head, your emotions and your thoughts. It doesn't mean you have to believe in a shopping trolly full of stuff you can't get your head around before you even start. Spiritual work is about you working with yourself, here and now in this place, at this time. Looking around at what there is, and trying to work out what it's all about. That's what people mean when they say 'spiritual'. It's not about 'spirit realms' and fairy kingdoms and trying to make yourself feel funny with or without strange substances; it's about us being alive in this place and time and trying to make sense of it. We want to see what it means because we're humans. Humans want to know what everything means. It's how we work. That's why we keep asking questions like 'Who am I?' and 'Why am I here?' and 'What's it all about?

What Religions are for

Religions are to help you find out what it's all about. They supply a ready-made, culturally-tailored set of ideas and pictures and metaphors to make sense of everything. In our times there are great cultural changes happening all over the world very quickly. In the Western world many people can no longer get their heads around religion, and think it's all very silly. This is fair enough, because some bits of religions, when you take them outside into the clear light of day, can look a bit silly. (I'm not going to single anything out here, because very religious people can sometimes get very excited about things, and I wish to have a quiet life, thank you very much.) That doesn't mean the whole premise of religion is silly. Because humans tend to be naturally spiritually inclined. Now 'spirituality' as a word, when you give it a good boiling down, doesn't mean much more than 'wanting to find out what everything means'. So many people use the word in so many ways it's ended up not meaning very much anymore. So where the word is used in this book, it doesn't mean you have to imagine loads of things, it means you have to stop imagining, and try to find out what's really there. Religions can actually help.

Science

Science has found out a lot of stuff that's really there. Galaxies and microbes and DNA, molecules and radioactivity and genetics and so forth. Which is great. I like that. What science tends to lack is that element of 'What does it mean?' that humans like so much. Scientists say: 'Look at all the big long numbers and the fancy names. Be impressed and relax. Could we please have another grant to do some more research over here?' And things like that. But science is essentially descriptive, it describes what exists and tries to find out how it works and fits together. That's good, but it doesn't satisfy the need that many people have in their lives to find out: (a) what it all means in general; and (b) what it all means for them personally. Humans live personal, individual lives, and science doesn't do personal and individual very well, and tends to avoid it. (Except in the general area of grants.)

Spirituality

So if you want to find out what it all means in general, and what it all means for you personally, spirituality is your only man. That means you might have to look at religion all over again, if you haven't been in the habit of doing so for a while. Many people reading this book may be religious already, and quite happy in their faith, and fair play to them. They know what they're doing. But others may be just perusing this book to see what it's about, and might be interested in revisiting a faith they were once brought up in, or which they've heard of. Or indeed they might be still in a faith, but are finding it hard going at the minute, and need a gee up. So this book is for those people, really.

I'm a Christian, and I'm writing this book from that viewpoint, but I do realise and understand that there are other ways of understanding the world and existence and matters of faith, so I'm trying to leave space for other people to feel included. That's not how Christians, or indeed people with a faith of any kind always behave, but I think it's a good idea. So I'm talking here in general about how we can use a mountain as a spiritual aid to explore ourselves and our existence and try to make a bit of sense of it for ourselves.

GOD!

The word 'God' has already been used quite a bit in this book, and it's probably time to sort out what it means. God is a very, very short word for something we don't understand and can't say much about. There are many ideas of who or what God is, and some people nowadays think they don't make sense, so they insist there isn't a God. Which is silly. They don't know any more than anyone else. They just have an opinion. The Buddha once said that people with opinions just go around arguing with other people with opinions. Opinions are just ideas, notions that we have, and we think are right. They may or may not be, but we hold them to be true. Science tries to step aside from opinion and prove things, which is good, and it is a principle that religious people should take on board. Except you can't prove or disprove most religious stuff, largely speaking, including God. What you can do, at the very least, is see what it means in itself and what way it's intended to make you think and see the world, and find out where that will take you. The point is to trust and explore the idea, rather than simply dismiss it because you don't understand it first time around.

Many of the things we are asked to believe in religions aren't there just because they're weird and wonderful and will impress slack-jawed punters of little brain, they are really there to cause or help us to think in certain ways; they are flavourings, influences, to affect how we behave and perceive the world. They are frequently embedded in story form. This can be a simple factual retelling of an event which happened, or it may also be something to help us think in a new way, to gain a certain understanding and insight without going into deep complicated theological explanations which we mightn't understand anyway. Stories are used as a simple way of getting ideas and concepts, perceptions and insights across without too much fuss. A way of carrying meaning in nice, memorable packaging.

You can see (me being a Christian and all) that I'm all for this God business. But I may not think there's a God the way you think I think I do, if you see what I mean. Many people say to me they don't believe in God. I ask them what sort of God they don't believe in. After they've told me, I can frequently cheerfully confess to them that I don't believe in that sort of a God either. Which can cause some confusion. (Confusion is good by the way. Confusion means that some sort of thinking and clarification might be about to happen, and that's not a bad thing.)

God is not simple. God is not the big, jolly, Santa-in-a-nightdress-in-the-sky character that many of us were sold when we were children. If God came up with the entirety of existence, then God has to be a bit more complicated than that.

Sensible religious people say the less you say about God the better, because most of what we end up saying about God is nonsense. (That rarely stops people trying, though!) There are some labels for God which are good because they actually show how little we understand about God, unlike the word 'God', which everyone thinks they understand; labels like: 'The Ground of Being' or 'the Ground of Becoming'. Or what God himself is reported to have said in the Bible when Moses asked him what his name was: 'I am that I am.' They say enough to stimulate and intrigue without pretending they are the whole of the answer. They inveigle us into thinking rather than just accepting, or assuming we know what's being talked about. Something like God doesn't fit inside words very well, and so the words can lead us astray.

The sort of magic-superman God, the anthropomorphic picture of God we see in parts of the Bible, is there because we have to think about God in some way, and humans are the smartest (on a good day) things we know about. But that's just a picture, a concept to point towards some sort of reality which is in a totally different ballpark. The name 'God' is actually only a label on the outside of a very, very big box of ideas that need careful consideration and sorting through, always bearing in mind that none of the ideas or concepts are actually it, or even get close. They're only pointing towards the greater reality which God is. You're going to have to do that sort of work yourself, I haven't room to do it for you here. And finding out is what spirituality, the spiritual quest, the Way, is all about.

Jesus

As a Christian, I think that at the very least we can say that Jesus Christ had a deep personal insight into the nature of God, the nature of reality, and tried to give it to other people. That's what his teachings and his life pointed to all the time. He called it the kingdom of God, and it was central to what he taught. His life, as we find it in the gospels, is an illustration of the nature of the kingdom, an illustration of Christ's insight into reality, into God and into himself. Jesus is a personification of the sacred. The episodes and stories which go to make up the gospels are carefully chosen to provide those insights to us as well. They're not just, or not even, nice wee stories we have to believe, they are primarily there to teach us stuff. You have to open the stories up and look inside them.

So, what about this mountain, then?
You can use a mountain like a spiritual tin opener to let some light into your mind and heart. It's just an aid. When you go up a mountain with a spiritual intent, with all your senses open and quietened, then it's like walking up into the sky and being suspended for a while between heaven and earth, in a manner of speaking. If you do it the right way, you can open up a gap and allow yourself to peer between worlds and perceptions; you can stand in the blurred place between human concepts and opinions, and reality. If you ascend the mountain in mind and heart and body, it can be an act of pure spirit. An act of deep meaning and insight.

Sacredness
The mountain is called holy or sacred sometimes. Now if you read the chapter on the history of Cruach Phádraig, you'll see there are lots of layers to it: Christian and pre-Christian, rituals and stories, gods, saints and demons. But that's not what makes the mountain sacred. All that is more human labelling and association. Whoever goes up the mountain will tend to

bring their own bundle of ideas and notions about what they expect to find at the top. Crom Dubh or Lugh, a vengeful Jehovah or a loving Christian God, or no God at all. But the truth that exists at the top of the mountain is beyond and above our opinions and imaginings, our words and definitions, all the ideas we project onto what we want to find.

That which is truly there, that which is the point, and reason and meaning and continuation of our being and existence, is there despite us talking and thinking, and in spite of our opinions. Reality exists however we see it, or twist it, or whatever colour we paint it. It is to see that reality, reflected and projected in ourselves, that we can climb the mountain. Reality is at the bottom of the mountain as well, but the ascent can bring a change of perception; stepping over or into a special boundary makes it clearer, strips away the usual trimmings. It can give us a chance to see, experience, take it on board. But only if we want to, try to and intend to.

Boundaries
Boundaries were always important in the old traditions in Ireland. The times between birth and baptism, between engagement and marriage, between death and burial were seen as being grey boundary areas in a human life in the old way of thinking. Here things become blurred; they are not this, that or the other. Cracks exist between the solid paving stones of our lives, where things might go awry, where forces outside us might change things. The in-between places of the year were viewed in the same way, where change happened, where the great feasts celebrated the swing of the earth around the sun. Imbolg and Bealtaine, Lúnasa and Samhain. Special places in nature were sacred too, because they were neither one thing nor the other. Where three rivers meet, for example,

bun na dtrí uisce, is held to be a special place, where enmity can be buried, sickness left behind. Where three waters come together is a crack, a gap in the world, so the same rules don't apply there. Places like this were a boundary, a threshold. A limen, where one thing passes over into another, and so there is a chink between the two things, the two concepts. Where a spring of clear water bubbles up from nowhere has the same special thing about it. Such wells become holy, attract the attention and names of saints, gather stories and the reputation of healings and blessings. This is one reason why a mountain, neither earth nor sky, reaching up into eternity, scraping the bellies of stars, can become the home of the gods, the way to heaven, the signpost to infinity and eternity. It is a place set apart, and different things can perhaps happen there. Perhaps we can learn to see reality, glimpse the kingdom of God that Jesus speaks of, for surely these are the same thing in the end?

We are easily blinded by the obvious and the ordinary which are things we invent for ourselves. We take them up the mountain with us. It is so easy while on the climb to see only the swirling, soaking, freezing mist, and little else. Our experience can be of sore knees and feet and worry at the long climb down, shivering and shuddering behind a dripping boulder. Or we can enjoy the wonderful scenery on a good day. But you can't eat the scenery, as the natives of the rougher and more scenic bits of the west of Ireland will tell you. There is eating and drinking on the Reek, but not in the obvious. You have to look in another way, expect different things.

Mountains
Mountains and divinity are long and widely associated. Mount Fuji, Olympus, the Andes, the pyramids of Mexico and

Egypt and Mesopotamia, Mount Sumeru of the Buddhists, Horeb and Sinai. Over and over, the mountain is the place where divinity dwells or lurks or feasts, blows out fire and smoke, speaks and commands. The finger of stone pushing up into the sky points to something beyond, and our imaginations strain to take that in. A mountain is the biggest thing any of us will ever see, far, far bigger than anything else we experience in ordinary life, and of course it stands out in our imaginations as a special place, a place apart.

Mountains are dangerous, uninhabited, different from the flat places. They can stand for many things. They provide, in the midst of the plain, in the midst of ordinary life, a separation that can be physical, geographical, climatic, cultural, mental and also spiritual.

Mountains mark boundaries, between sky and earth, between the tectonic plates of our world. They can be wilderness for us, even when cultivated land laps far up their slopes. Even when paths cross them, sheep cluster on them, they are a place apart. A 'thinner' place, where one world seems nearer to another, where reality is stretched a bit, the envelope of our perceptions pushed out a bit more.

Concepts

We're inclined to nail down our own personal world with concepts, one after another. Words like 'ordinary', 'everyday', 'usual'. Names and ideas fix things solidly in the mental maps we've been drawing since childhood. We don't need to look anymore, we know the names and concepts so well the realities don't need to concern us and we can gloss over the detail of much of our experience. Seen one sparrow, one daisy, seen them all. We provide ourselves with a simple mental checklist, through culture and personal experience, to enable us to get on with our lives. So then the individual, the special, the idiosyncratic escapes us. We prefer the general to the specific, the generic to the unique. Once we 'know' what something is and have named it, we move on without inspection or experience of the moment. We live in a mental map rather than real physical geography. We prefer photography to actually looking, smelling, touching and remembering. We refer to the travel books of our mind instead of actually being where we are. It's like choosing television instead of having an actual life. As a result, our mental experience of the world is an apparently seamless panorama of safe, classified images, rolling on and on like a cleverly cut and edited film. But that is not reality. That is our mind providing a safe, classified, alternative experience.

Mental Movies
When we look more closely at what's going on inside our heads, we begin to see that the mental movie, which appears seamless, is really a patchwork of secondary experience and conceptualisation. Like a real physical piece of film, one snapshot, one idea comes after another. Slow the film down, and the meaningless, soothing automatic soundtrack of music and drivelled commentary we supply begins to lose its fascination, its sense. Then we begin to see that our minds are doing much of the work for us. As the speed of the film slows even more, the separate frames, one after another, one concept after another, begin to show up. Meditation can do this for us; it can begin to slow down our mind so that we can begin to see and understand it. It can give us the power of concentration and intense awareness so that we can begin to see stuff as it is, not as we believe it to be. We can slow down the thought process. See what we're doing. Perceive how we

perceive. Learn to understand and empathise with ourselves. Have compassion for ourselves as we truly are. Then with a bit of thought, we can learn to have compassion for others, since they just work the same way we do.

Mind the Gap!

When the thoughts come more slowly, when there are gaps between them, what's in those gaps? The answer is: reality. Unadorned and unadulterated by concepts, words and opinions. As I said earlier, reality is where God is. We're inclined to create a mental screen and display our thoughts and perceptions on it. God is always there, but we erect the screen in front of him. We blot him out, obscure him with images and ideas about him. Even sacred ideas blessed and hallowed by scripture, tradition and the Holy Church can be an obstruction between us and God. The commandment about 'graven images' extends even to mental graven images. They are not the real thing. The real thing exists only in reality.

Meditation doesn't get us closer to God. God is closer to all of us than our own skins already. But meditation and prayer allow the veils and screens to be pulled aside, so that we can begin to glimpse the reality behind them.

Who am I?

In the course of an ordinary life, we don't usually have experiences like this. One reason is that we think the flow of thoughts and pictures and drivel in our heads is us, and that that's all there is. We never doubt it. This little flurried fountain of automatic thought and emotion and opinion, for many of us, is our very soul. This is our secret, private personal core, and the very centre of our being. Only a little experimentation shows that we have little or no control over it. We aren't making it happen, and we cannot easily stop it happening. Something else is making these pictures, these judgments, these feelings, recycling these memories, humming that song over and over. Not us. We are not this process; because we can watch it, see its separateness from us, the gap between it and us. Our control over it is only temporary. Any attempt to stop thinking is doomed to failure. Have a go and see for yourself. This opinionated chatterer and whistler in the dark is your mind, a bundle of memories and ideas and habits and inclinations. It is not you. We identify with drivel, and ignore the true life in us. We identify with the objects of consciousness, the by-products, and are unconscious of consciousness itself.

The basic idea I'm getting at here is that we think too much and we believe our own publicity. There are ways to help us work with that, and when we do them, we find out what countless other people have found out; that there is a reality beyond all the thinking and ideas and concepts. In that reality is what I call God. We can help this process by going to places where things are different, where the concepts do not stick together so well, where boundaries are superseded, gaps exist between one thing and another; where there is silence and peace and emptiness and opportunity. This is one of the things that prayer, meditation, spirituality does for us, it provides the gap, the space, the calm that can let us see how we perceive and think and behave, and allow us to think and see differently.

People always used the boundary places. Or if they didn't have any handy, they built them. That's what cathedrals and churches and temples and mosques were for; they were to be places apart from ordinary life, places which would help you think and see in another way. Sacred or consecrated is the word we use for that. Where you can come up to the edge and look over.

Pilgrimage

We'll discuss pilgrimage in more detail in the next chapter, but suffice it to say here that pilgrimage in itself creates a boundary place, during the movement, the travel. It's outside of ordinary life; one temporarily becomes a traveller, a pilgrim, which is not an ordinary role in society. As pilgrims we are in a limenal space; no longer the usual routine of work/sleep/eat, but a less solid place, with a different order of events happening to us. We are taken to the edge of life, out of the main flow of the culture, the routine, the everyday. We are presented, through movement and distance, with the opportunity to perceive and live differently. Whether that pilgrimage involves miles of travel and real mountains, or is in our own back yard, is immaterial. We can access a new place to stand, from which we can see more clearly.

Self

The true reality which lies beyond our opinions and frantic thought is what gets called Spirit, or Reality, or Truth, or the Self, or God, or Allah, or the Great Void, or Buddha Mind. It is what most religions point to and deal with. It is where they are all hoping to go when they start out. Most faiths, Christianity included, are to do with seeing past the self (small s) and finding the Self, the larger reality, the place where God is. Most of us are fascinated with our own small, selfish worlds, we live and die without ever finding out that anything else exists outside our thoughts and opinions. Like oysters or barnacles, we spend our entire existence inside a shell, a life of our own creation, which is about us alone and what we desire or dislike. Spirituality is about us beginning to see and recognise this, and looking further to our connection with what really exists, outside what we think of as ourselves. This is talked about in terms of 'surrender' in Islam, 'extinguishing' in Buddhism and 'death' in Christianity, for example.

Die to Live

Jesus says we must die to have life. Whoever saves their life will lose it. Christian baptism is a symbol of dying and rising again, where part of us, the 'old us', dies. This is not our final physical death, it is a death within life, utter change, rebirth, wakening up from sleep and unconsciousness into what Christ calls more abundant life. That can only happen to us when we begin to look beyond the clutter of judgements, classifications and opinions our culture and upbringing have given us to think with. It can only happen when we look for the spaces between the comforting notions our minds come up with one after another. It is in the gaps that the Spirit can be glimpsed, at the edges of seemingly solid things, where one concept grades into another, clings to another. Spirit is behind all things, within all things, but it is not easy to *see* in things, until your eye comes in on it. Better to study the edges, where there is some chance of movement and flexibility, where we might catch a flash of some brightness that promises deeper meaning, where the massive tectonic plates of our conceptual view of the world might bang together, lurch and shift and show the reality they represent and conceal. Then we might glimpse that there are more dimensions to the world. Our ordinary existence, the one our minds supply us with, is more like a 2D cartoon. True 3D reality is out there, but we have to look to find it.

Life

Our lives are very packed places. There is too much going on. Work, sport, children, shopping, housekeeping. Even leisure can be a fraught activity. Spirituality is another claim on our time, and it gets pushed aside. All of which means we have to make the space, steal back the minutes, the hour or two, and redesignate, re-prioritise, rearrange. You have to actually do it on purpose. Not easy, harder again to do regularly, even harder to keep up from one season to another, one year to another. For all of us humans, spirituality and the practice of it has this amount of sameness about it: we have to do it on purpose; we have to take the time to do it; and we have to find a place to do it in. Not much grounds for world-shattering ecumenism and inter-religious cooperation there, you might think. In our Western world, though, those first steps are increasingly the ones that are missing, whatever about the details that come after.

This book is to try to help with that. Find your mountain, your hill, your lump, your special place and walk up it and down again, be in it or on it on purpose, in cold blood and in full consciousness of what you are doing. And make it spiritual. Never mind aerobic or relaxing or invigorating, welcome by-products though they might be. Make it a time to be with yourself, not with your worries and cares and pains and fears, but with what you actually are, who you really are. The you you were before they hoisted you into the world and called you names. Under the labels and ideas and everything else our culture slaps on top of you, and that you faithfully carry around with you all the time, and deeply, really believe in, is who you really are. That's the you that God loves.

Damp-bottomed Explorers

Once upon a time, we were all small, we couldn't talk, we had no names for things, no idea of what anything was. But all of us got there eventually; we pulled on the cloak of language and culture over our heads. And that is how we see and perceive and conceptualise the world, through that linguistic, cultural filter. But there is an older layer still there. Before we got the language trick worked out, we were putting every-thing we could lay our hands on into our mouths. We have tasted most things in our world. Some we'd probably not like to think about! Look around you. You know inherently what everything tastes like. A doorknob, the edge of a table, the leg of a chair, a coin; the flavours, the sensation on your tongue is still there for recall. The damp-bottomed explorers we once were had mapped the world out in tastes and textures. We could sing, even before we knew the words, in a sense.

So, never mind labels – before speech, before ideas and concepts, class and tribe and race, even before gender, we exist. Before we were even born, before our parents were born, we had a face. Spirituality is going back to that, and to the universe of which we are an intimately related part. Beyond that, beneath that, behind that, within and around it is the 'Ground of Existence', the whatever-it-is that holds the whole show in being, and brings it into life and light. I call that God, because I am a Christian. For you, there might be other names, other ideas, whatever your culture has bequeathed you. Perhaps our modern culture has left you nothing at all to work with, which is increasingly the case. Then be assured that what is called by many names is welcoming, and that you are already a part of it. It is open for you to explore and experi-ence.

Religions
Religions have a bad press in Western culture. Spirituality is the up and coming thing we are told. But spirituality can be merely a plastic pastiche of the old religions stripped of

structure and direction and checks and balances. This is spiritual cherry picking, where someone looks for the bits that feel good and taste nice and are bright and cheery and fit handily into a paperback book and will offend no one. Or possibly do much good either, except for the author. But the great world faiths have upsides and downsides, dark and light, pain and pleasure built into them. They mirror and reveal and reflect the world, and are connected to it, because they are about real things, not just 'feeling good'. They have been around for a while, they are the way they are because people have used them over and again, polished and developed them. Their structures reflect something in reality, and don't just consist of the edited highlights and detached techniques we can be presented with by enterprising authors. The older traditions have many facets, not all of them 'nice'. There is a hard, sharp penitential edge to them that some modern-day writers of self-help books would rather ignore. That hard edge reflects facets of ourselves, of godhood, that may not be fashionable nowadays in our culture, but that can't simply be edited away.

That doesn't mean that the older religions can't ever be criticised, or never need to be renewed by fresh perceptions. The only religions that spark no enthusiastic discussions are dead ones. Jesus himself was seen as criticising the Jewish religion and its wider culture as it was practised and perceived at the time. When he spoke from a new standpoint – the kingdom of God – he was only doing what the prophets before him did. We are called to that as well. Christ's criticism of the religious culture of his day is just as applicable to our own. Spirituality, the search for meaning, entering into the kingdom of God, is still relevant today, still has things to show us. Spiritual insight always needs to be refreshed and re-embodied in new words and concepts for each new generation, and in response to cultural change. This would be at the very least to preserve any faith from the slow, natural process that tends to convert them into mindless habit and unconsidered cultural customs through time. Religions die when they don't make sense any more, don't resonate with people's lives, when the wisdom gets lost because the rituals seem empty and the words have no meaning.

Meaning

Spirituality is to do with meaning and the search for it, and though we might find different words or concepts to express that meaning, we are all in search of it. Our modern commercial culture would like us to think that we don't need to bother, because we know how a washing machine works, for example. We can explain stuff, we can understand a bit about very basic science, we have a vague idea about genetics, astronomy, anatomy and medicine, and meaning seems besides the point. So eat this, drink this, buy that and drive this and never mind about meaning. We listen to the message, we believe it, and everything seems well and good.

When, once upon a time, we didn't live as long, or weren't as warm or well fed, meaning was important. Now everything tends to be reduced to a utilitarian level of financial worth and mechanical relationship. But 'why?' hasn't gone away, whether we like it or not. When death or illness appears, or things go wrong in our ordered lives, it becomes clear to most people that there is more to this existence than material wealth, and that science doesn't, can't, explain everything about us. Spirituality is the only way to find out, to begin to understand and see clearly who we are, and what our life actually is, at some deeper level.

'Why?' is inbuilt; it comes as part of our intelligence. It isn't an optional build-on accessory; we are born with it. Anti-religion authors may bewail the meme that parasitises us, or the mental deficiency we are born with that makes us look for meaning in things, but it is still part of us, part of how we tick. We tell stories, we make stories; one thing has to lead to another, and back to something else. Effects have causes which have effects, and on and on. We like to look for them, trace them, follow them, and not just that, we want to know why it is the way it is, what it all means. Meaning is the deep, deep resonance of how humanity understands the world, under-stands itself. Meaning is the internal chamber, the radical wellspring where religion, spirituality, art, music, literature, creativity all resonate. We are not human without those things. We are not calm, dispassionate observers, the stance scientists try to take. Humans are actually, personally involved at the level of heart and head. Our lives are on the line, not theories. We are not observers, we are participants, causations, effects, victims, winners and losers, we act and are acted upon. Even as spectators, we are affected. We are part of it, and we want to know what it's all about, and who or what is to blame, and would they please stop? (Or do it again, if we really liked it!)

More Mountainy Stuff

We can ascend the Holy Mountain both in a physical and a spiritual sense, and begin to explore who we are, where we come from, and the nature of the universe, the life, in which we exist. The mountain is a metaphor and a device, a special place somewhere, or just inside our own heads. The place where God is. Where Jesus went when he prayed. We can go there too.

So. Go find a mountain.

Pilgrimage

Pilgrimage is the physical act of travelling with a spiritual, religious intent, usually to a special, sacred place. At the same time, it can also be seen metaphorically as representing our path through life, from birth to death, or our spiritual path towards God. So in one sense we are all pilgrims, all travelling, all heading towards something special. We are all (as it says somewhere) 'sojourners'. This is not our home, any of us, wherever we are. We're just on the way through. Even realising this begins to make us think differently, see ourselves differently. Pilgrimage is a way of thinking.

Travelling itself doesn't necessarily make us into a pilgrim. A trip, even to the Holy Land or some shrine or other, can be just pure tourism, a holiday, and that's ok. But pilgrimage is a mental state, an intention. It requires preparation and thought and prayer. It may be done for one specific reason or intention, or simply as something spiritual that's good for you. When you are on pilgrimage, it's a time to pray, to think differently, see in fresh ways, get a new angle on the world and on yourself in it. It is, above all, a time to be with God. A time set aside and spent with God.

Historically, pilgrimage is one of the neutral religious technologies common all over the earth in many faiths. It is even built into Islam as an integral part of that religion. In Christianity, it began as people wished to go to the Holy Land to see for themselves the places where the events of the gospels actually happened. Buddhists, Hindus and others also have pilgrimage as part of their religion.

Pilgrimage in Ireland

For Christians, Jerusalem or Rome was the place to go. Jerusalem for obvious reasons, and Rome had the relics of major saints like Paul and Peter, and was the centre of the Western Christian Church. For many centuries either journey was perilous. The chances of returning, or even arriving at all, were slim. Indeed such pilgrimages were placed on people as severe penances in the case of particularly heinous sins. The time and resources necessary for making such a long journey also meant that few people were able to undertake it. So people travelled to the nearest sacred places available to them. Somewhere where a special relic was kept, for example, or a holy well, or places associated with saints and holy persons from past generations, or indeed the older pagan places of assembly, which became Christianised over the centuries, like the Reek. Ordinary people with few resources could at least spare a couple of days to walk to a special, holy place not too far from them.

In Ireland, the Reek, or 'Patrick's Purgatory' in Lough Derg in Co. Donegal were famous even outside Ireland in medieval Europe. At the same time, the unsettled nature of the country during most of her history worked against the growth of major pilgrimages. The pilgrimages mentioned above did draw numbers, but not on a scale comparable to the rest of Europe. The emphasis in most of Ireland was on the local.

72

Ireland is a very concentrated place. Every small area has its own dialect and traditions, its own patchwork of meaning and ritual, and also its own facilities for pilgrimage, healing, and congregation. Holy wells and sacred sites, ancient churches, Christianised pagan places and artefacts, a saint or two, traditions enough to facilitate the local population without them having to go too far. Pilgrimage need not involve huge distance, travel and danger. It may be a couple of nights away from home, something or somewhere in the locality which facilitates devotion and quietness, and allows a space apart. Every small area of Ireland had such unofficial devotional facilities, and still does, though many have fallen from use.

People were moved to travel to these places for personal spiritual reasons, but also to repeat and reinforce the collective, communal meanings that gave sense to their existence. This wasn't necessarily a totally solemn, serious business. It was also festival and celebration, social and religious, political, medical, educational and formed and perhaps defined the community. It was part of being alive, of being human. It still is.

The Real Thing

People have a need to touch, to contact, the real thing. Whether it was the physical relics of a holy person, or a place associated with them, people wanted, and still want to be close to the real thing, the thing that works. Our God is invisible and intangible, but we have a need in us for things we can physically experience. Saintly people are as near as most of us can get.

The first we hear of relics in Christianity is from the Acts of the Apostles (19:11): 'God did extraordinary miracles through Paul, so that when the handkerchiefs or aprons that had touched his skin were brought to the sick, their diseases left them, and the evil spirits came out of them.' The tombs and bones of early Christian martyrs also gathered an aura around them. If you can't get to the real thing itself, Jesus, God, the Apostle Paul or some other certified saintly person, then something which they had touched, or even better, a part of their physical remains was seen as being a good substitute. Whether it was a splinter of wood possibly from the True Cross, a piece of a saint's body, their clothes or belongings, the places where their relics were kept, or where the traditions about them were strongest, acquired a reputation for being 'special'.

The physical places themselves may be remarkable; wells and rivers, mountains and hills, cliffs and rocks. On the other hand it might be just the stories attached to a perfectly ordinary-looking place. Somewhere where something is supposed to have happened in a previous time can be enough. People feel that perhaps this place is one where things did happen, can happen, and perhaps something will happen again. So they go to see, in the hope that the real thing might be available to them there.

Thin Places
Then there's the idea of there being 'thin' places in the world, where we are closer to another reality, a different world. From an earlier religious stratum in Ireland, we have places reputed to be gates to the Underworld; mounds and raths inhabited by a separate parallel race, visible only exceptionally, abodes of gods and spirits, or places where they are more concentrated in themselves, easier to imagine, to contact, to be influenced and beguiled. Places where favours might be granted, miracles dispensed and cures acquired from the

largesse of Providence. Christianity, as in the case of the Reek, took many of these places over, and christened them.

My own inclination would be to say that these are places apart, not frequented in the usual round of life, and they allow us to step outside that round for a while. They do have the potential of bringing us closer to another world, but not one from a science fiction film or fantasy novel. This other world is the true world, the reality where God is, hidden and obscured from us by our own thinking and opinions. The special places allow us to set those thoughts and opinions to one side, and be in the presence of reality, and inhabit it fully. If we're lucky we might be able to bring a bit of it away with us.

To go to holy places, to pray at them, can begin to initiate a relationship, the possibility of our connecting to something outside us. The universe, other beings around us, and God himself. This is a learning curve. It is rarely what we expect it to be. This is also what pilgrimage is really about. It is a microcosmic lifetime, a small spiritual hothouse which can help to fast-track us in our personal spiritual development and journey.

Most religions are not just about how to relate to God, but also how to relate to other people and to ourselves; how to make sense of the world and where we are within it. One implies the other. The Summary of the Law found in three of the gospels is a good way of putting it: Love God with all your heart and soul and mind, and love your neighbour as yourself. Love for God, love for neighbour and love for yourself. Developing each one of those kinds of love is an art in itself, and that's what spirituality can bring out in us. Prayer, meditation and other religious practices are designed to help us change, grow up, mature in love and in God and in ourselves. It takes time, and thought and effort and application.

It doesn't necessarily mean you have to believe more than six impossible things before breakfast, but you will have to put the work in.

Doing the Work

Pilgrimage is one way to do the work. There are things to learn from all parts of it, not just being in the special place. The going and the coming are as important as the somewhere. By taking the time out, you are already *in* a special place, not ordinary life, not work or children or shopping or TV. You will have created a gap, a space, in which things can happen. It may be only half a day going up and down the mountain, or it may be six weeks tramping the Camino. The weight of ordinary concerns are taken off our heads so that we can grow upwards, expand to fill the whole space of ourselves. Pilgrimage changes our concerns from the usual daily round to new, more immediate ones. Food and sleeping and rain and sun and sore feet. It changes horizons, brings a healthy freshening physicality into the whole business.

You can go on a pilgrimage entirely on your own. That's a big thing to do. All of us should do it at one stage in our lives if we get the chance. People have discovered that the Camino, for example, is a place where you can get your head 'steam cleaned' internally, meet people, and have something out of the ordinary and perhaps spiritual happen to you. There are as many different reasons for doing it as there are people walking on it. Some people do it for the old reasons still – because the relics of St James are in Compostela, and they are going to pray there. The same with Croagh Patrick. Of the thousands going up for more than a look around and a day out, there are many reasons in many hearts for the trip. But more people do it with an intention which is directed towards something, spiritual growth or maturity or experimentation, or the answer to questions. Or to leave space to learn to live with a bereavement, a loss, a hurt, a threat, an illness. Time just to be with God and with yourself. Those are good reasons that can bring more lasting results.

Ah, Now!
Now! It does have to be said, as it has been said before, in this case in a marginal note in a ninth century Irish hymnbook: 'Going to Rome involves great effort and little reward, for the King whom you seek there you will not find unless you bring him with you.' (Johnathan Sumption, *Pilgrimage*, p. 98) This was possibly a criticism of Rome, but has more wisdom in it than just that!

Also: 'You may learn more and travel farther by just staying at home instead of traipsing about the place.' Someone important probably said that, I forget who. (Someone will probably tell me.)

In the first case, as I've mentioned already, God is as much at the bottom of the mountain as he is at the top. As Jung said, 'Bidden or unbidden, God is present.' This is a comfort to many people in itself. No problem there. But finding God in the here and now is something most people have to learn. It's not easy to make it real, to realise it. We can do it by luck or force of will for a moment or two sometimes. Some people might even call that a religious experience; but to sustain it, to live with God and in God, is not easy. Our minds rebel at the intrusion on our privacy and personal space, the apparent restriction it implies. To achieve a state where we accept God's presence, trust in it being there, assume it and give welcome space to it within our own lives and existence, takes a bit of practice. It is the chief ideal and goal of Christian spirituality; to live constantly in that place where God is, the place Jesus called the kingdom of God. It is here and now, but not quite; still to be consummated, but yet present and available. In us, with us, amongst us and around us. Reality itself. So we use spiritual techniques to help us get there, help us to learn to live there. Prayer and meditation, the Holy Eucharist, reading and thinking and discussion with other people. All of it helps, all of it moves us a bit further on in the road.

Pilgrimage is one of those techniques. It is one which may suit some more than others, but can be good for all. Perhaps, sometimes, we need to move away, physically away, to find God, to see reality. We need to step out of our old shoes, our old tracks and find new ones. This is what mountains and sacred places are good for, what they're used for by humans. Places apart, thin places, out of the ordinary places. Places of meaning where meaning might be found. Places where you can see clearly for miles and miles from a good vantage point, both life and landscape. Then you can reassess and understand in a true, wide perspective, in contrast to the tight, narrow place you may have felt your life to be. That's what a pilgrimage is for, what the Reek is for, the Camino, Mount Brandon, Lough Derg, Sceilig Mhichíl, Jerusalem.

Staying at Home
In the second case, pilgrimage can, of course, be purely internal; you don't have to physically move, to go places. Pilgrimage is a mindset, not necessarily a geographical re-location. We can stay in our metaphorical monastic cells, and travel within ourselves, within our own lives. Such a metaphorical pilgrimage can be hard to sustain in the long term. That's what monastic communities were and are for, but it is also true that that is what local churches are for, that's what the Eucharist is for, to provide community, companionship, food for the journey of life shared together. A bunch

of like-minded people moving through their lives together. Help and support to sustain a spiritual life, a personal pilgrimage with others. If you're not physically able to go on a pilgrimage, or don't have the time or opportunity, then begin to think in this way of your life, your time. Take the perspective of journeying, learning, seeing what's around the next corner, and moving through all this with God, in God, and by God's grace, whatever comes. Pilgrimage is a metaphor, a microcosm of real life. By going away to do it we just ramp up the intensity a bit, sharpen the focus.

A Retreat on Two Legs

A pilgrimage is really a retreat on two legs. 'Retreat' can be a scary concept, depending on what was inflicted on you in your past under that name, perhaps at school. It may have the associations of long hours of silence, loneliness, boredom, hard work, cold, lack of sleep and bad food or even (non-optional!) fasting. If you didn't really want to be there, then it can't have been much fun. Or much use, either. Pilgrimage, on the other hand, will be purely voluntary. You don't have to go unless you want to. You're a grown up now, you can make your own decisions, you're in charge. It will get you out of the house, do you good; it involves walking about (at least a bit, if you can) and there are spiritual benefits.

Other Human Beings

Pilgrimages are done frequently in a group with other people, which has upsides and downsides, as is the way with people. Living in a pilgrim community can be a learning experience in itself. (Have a read at Chaucer's *Canterbury Tales* and see!) A group provides support and help. They can also be a pure torture to be going around with. The proximity of other people when one is tired or stressed makes getting on with them more complicated, harder. Small things rub us as raw as the blisters on our feet. We feel more, see more than we would in our ordinary minds. But that's good for us as well. We may learn more than just what we wanted or expected to learn about human nature, especially our own! There is much opportunity here for letting others teach us about ourselves, by just watching ourselves and our reactions. Trying to understand where the feelings and impulses come from within ourselves.

Why?
What makes a pilgrimage different from a good walk? Intention. The intention to go for a certain reason. That reason will be personal to you. There are many possible reasons: spiritual growth is probably the greatest, but there's also giving thanks, looking for physical or mental healing, recompense, penance, forgiveness, or mourning.

You can do a pilgrimage for yourself, of course, but you can also do it for someone else. You can dedicate any benefits to another person. Now, whether this makes a difference to them is not a question with a simple answer, but it will certainly make a difference to you. It may bring closure and healing to you as a result of a relationship which went wrong, for example. It's a bit like forgiveness, which is a close comparison. Forgiving someone is always good for us, but it may or may not make a difference to the other person. We may lay down the burden of hatred or guilt or pain we carry, and which only does us harm, but the other person may not wish to know, may not accept our forgiveness or even realise the need of it. We may not even be able to talk to them, or tell them that we have forgiven them. So the results we can only ever see in ourselves for definite. Any other results, in a strange way, aren't our business. That doesn't mean they don't exist.

Buddhists talk about 'sharing merit'. This is where any benefits derived from meditation or spiritual practices are shared in a short prayer of intent with all living or all sentient beings in existence. Who knows what the results of that are? But the obvious lesson it teaches in generosity, sharing, and selflessness outweighs any perceivable benefits. Christ taught us about self-sacrifice, sharing, giving, accepting. Rather than seeking benefits for ourselves, we can share our spiritual labours with others, with all sentient beings in existence! Someone very smart (probably Mahatma Gandhi) once said, 'You must be the change you wish to see in the world.'

Devotion, Penance or Thanksgiving

People need to do something concrete, sometimes. Words and thoughts alone can seem of little use. A time comes when we feel we have to physically demonstrate our feelings and wishes. When someone dies or falls ill, for example, people around have a strong urge to do something, anything, to help in some way. Statements and offers of help and intentions don't feel like enough. It is a great grace for those affected to allow people to do small things for them. Physical action is sometimes the only thing which can bring relief, make the feelings and intentions real and concrete, bring closure and consummation.

On the positive side, great joy energises us, fills us with something that needs expression, sometimes in more than words. So does great gratitude, relief, or in a more religious sense, the strong need to show response to God, perhaps coming from a level within us deeper than words can express or show. Pilgrimage can fulfil this role for people. It can be one way for them to express and show forth devotion, love, adoration beyond words and mechanically repeated praises, and live it through physical, prayerful movement and an existence devoted for a while to living for God alone.

Penance

Penance is no longer a very fashionable topic in Christian religious circles, but it is worth thinking about. As a simplistic punishment for sin, a jail sentence to be mechanically served, it may be of little worth. Looked at as a joyful response to absolution and forgiveness, as a lived out expression of a restored, trusting and trustful relationship with God, with the world and with other people, then it can have value in it. Pilgrimage can be a worthwhile expression of this, marking the line in the sand between one life and another, allowing space for the changing of habits and thought patterns, and growing new ways of looking at ourselves and at the world.

It is perhaps more productive to think of penance as a way to grow remorse rather than guilt. Remorse results in the positive response of 'repentance': a turning towards a new way of living and thinking, a turning towards the way of growth. It is a turning against the stream of culture and habit. It is a recognition of wrongdoing, but it is a positive emotion, providing a ground within which change can grow. It lets light in. Guilt is remaining in the dark, re-remembering the pain, the shame, the anger. Guilt is self-directed anger which stunts growth and restricts change rather than encourages it; it keeps the light out. Guilt has little movement or development promised within it. Pilgrimage can provide the space, allow a chink where light might shine in and repentance happen. A period of time where thoughts can return to the problem in a constructive way without being crowded out, or masked by the demands of ordinary living. Done prayerfully and spiritually, penance can be a door to wisdom that will strengthen and nurture the changes we desire to see within ourselves. A chance to look at our lives, to examine and understand, witness and observe, with compassion, kindness and understanding. Not judging but loving, as our God does with us.

Gratitude

Pilgrimage can be a means of giving thanks: of making a sacrifice, a thank-offering of a piece of our life and time and existence and giving it to God, sharing it with him. This can be a reasonable, sensible response to some great grace felt to have been received, not in repayment but in acknowledgement and recognition. The sacrifice is not given away, we are not lessened by it. Rather it is shared by us with God. As in the Eucharist, all we have comes from God, all we are comes from God, all we give is God's already, but the physical act can mean more and have more effect on us than words and intentions. Anyway, some of us aren't word people. We like to do stuff, move, use our hands, make things, get up and be active. Pilgrimage can fulfil those of us who are that way inclined, as well as the word people who like to talk, who like words and sentences, prayers and readings.

Grief

Pilgrimage can also have a role to play in grief and bereavement. We can do it in thanks, in memory, as a way of keeping the departed in prayer in our hearts. But more directly, as a way of working through the inevitable grief and pain that come with the loss of one dear to us. I would recommend though that anything like this be done in the company of others, and perhaps with the advice and help of a trained counsellor.

Meeting God

On pilgrimage, we get the chance to meet God, to meet Christ in new and deeply personal ways. It may be in our fellow travellers, or in those we meet on the way up or down. It may be in our own hearts and minds. It may be in the wind, or rain or sun, or the sights before our eyes. It may be the feeling of just being alive, just existing and breathing and moving. It may be in the words of scripture or liturgy and prayer. It may be through breath, through silence, through our beating heart. In this time apart, at this gap between worlds which is neither earth nor sky, in this small piece of our life, given freely to God, we may freely receive.

Young People

Young people take easily to pilgrimage. The chance of time away, travel, being out in the air is attractive. They take more easily than adults to new things, even new rules and ways of behaving. Young people and children are better at playing, pretending, reimaging themselves. Adults can chafe and complain. But, when it is presented in the right way, children and young people can gain a lot from time out spent in a spiritual way, more than we might give them credit for at first thought. They are in a time of fast change and growth, and pilgrimage can have a special meaning for them. They are sensitive to atmosphere and intuitively understand the concepts of 'special' and 'sacred'. Meditation comes to them more easily than adults, though concentration spans may be shorter and other styles of meditation may be necessary, but they have fewer barriers and preconceptions and worries than many adults would. Pilgrimage, handled sensitively and well, can be a painless, effective way in to a faith world from which modern youth culture has become very distant, and to which it is to some extent hostile.

Pilgrimage can provide the stepping stone for beginning a new life, or a new way of living the life we have. It can draw a line in the sand for us, take us away from the daily grind for long enough for us to reassess and understand it for what it is, and come back with a fresh approach and perspective. Pilgrimage can provide time to think. But it can also provide time not to think! We spend so much time caught up in ordinary considerations, worrying, planning, reminiscing, just our ordinary lives crowding in on us, that it's good to take time to just be. To breathe and walk and look around us, feel wind and sun and the path beneath our feet. Give our brains a rest, and allow a space to develop in them in which God can be with us and we with God. In the silence. That's what mantra meditation is for, that's why we count breaths, concentrate on footfalls, the movement and sensation of legs and body. To slow down and gradually fade out the talk and singing and worry and drivel and replaying of old mental videos and memories and fantasies, and allow space for truth, in God's name.

CHAPTER SIX

Prayer

Devote yourselves to prayer,
keeping alert in it with thanksgiving.
(*Colossians 4:2*)

These next two chapters deal with the basics of praying and meditating. Of course there's much more to it than just this. You can ascend to great heights on the spiritual mountain, so to speak, through prayer and meditation. These chapters are only to get you started off on the small bumps at the base. Indeed it may feel for a while that you are only mucking about in the car park at the bottom, rather than ascending any spiritual mountain at all. But learning skills takes time and patience, and the basics of prayer or meditation are a skill like anything else. Concentration and discipline at the very least. Once you acquire the basics, once it begins to become familiar, and you know your way about, then there are other things you can do and try. But this is somewhere to begin.

So, where would you start?

The first stage underlying any prayer life, any course of meditation, is morality. This is not seen as a 'cool' thing in our culture, unfortunately. The modern world hasn't much time for the idea, and it appears to be a very negative and forbidding concept. Perhaps it's more easily understood and accepted if it's put as 'right living'. What's the best way to live our lives? What's the best path to follow that produces the most happiness, does the least harm, and is good for us and for the other people we come in contact with? That's what morality is about. Learning how to do that, and understanding it at a deep level is called wisdom. Wisdom grows naturally from prayer and meditation.

Morality is not what most people in our culture would see as being the starting place for doing a course in prayer or meditation. They would expect to go straight in to exercises and practices, and a few explanatory talks, and off you go. Meditation tends to be seen as being about relaxation, stress reduction, or strange experiences. But prayer and meditation involve your mind and heart, the very core of your being. If those aren't in a good way, then it is hard to get a level foundation to build on. All of us, without exception, have imbalances and strong currents within us, coming from fears and dislikes, desires and needs, and we need to be aware of them. Those personal rocks are the ones you'll hit first. How you are living is important. Being able to *see* how you are living is important so that you can be in balance within yourself and with the people around you. Prayer and meditation can help you achieve that balance, but you must be aware of needing it in the first place before you start.

Living in the real world, in the kingdom of God, or indeed morality, isn't so much a matter of obeying rules and following laws – doing so will only get you so far – rather, it is a way of thinking and seeing outlined, implied, described by the laws and rules. It's more a matter of love, care, compassion and attention than 'not doing stuff', which is how morality is often thought of. Right living is about emphasising the positive rather than just condemning the negative. All the commandments and precepts of all the faiths are about ways of living with those around us (including God), and living with ourselves. They are about the very nature and kind of us at the deepest level.

So it is no harm to sit down quietly some time, in cold blood, and look at yourself, your relationships, your life, where it's coming from and where it's going to. Be honest, but also gentle and kind with yourself. What needs to be fixed? What isn't going well? What makes you feel ashamed, unhappy? What's not good? Most of us have a pretty good idea of all this if we could take the time to sit down with ourselves and review it honestly. On the other hand we also need to look at what *is* good and positive in your life, what is a blessing, what makes you feel good about yourself? What do you do right? Again, it's all pretty obvious, but sometimes you have to look at it on purpose to realise it's there, rather than take it for granted. People are also most likely to highlight the bad bits and downplay the good bits of themselves. Be aware of that.

It is frequently recommended that you do this daily, perhaps at the same time each day. Reviewing the day before going to sleep, perhaps. It is how we can become aware of the reality of our lives, the deep truth of them, and of who we really are. Not so that we can beat ourselves up, but so we can learn about ourselves, and look where we're going rather than walk blindly along. It is to feed and inform change within us. We can and should involve God in all this as part of our prayer life, even though it's true that God knows all about it already!

The 'confession' is of more benefit to us than God, to teach us about ourselves and our lives. So while you're about all this, try to begin to understand yourself. How you tick, how you think. Where do the habits kick in, where are you not conscious or aware of what you're saying or doing at the time, what makes you react, be angry, be happy or sad. Begin to get to know yourself, not with condemnation, or even with obligatory 'positive affirmation', but as clearly and truly as you can. Use the acceptance, mercy and love with yourself that you see mirrored in the eyes of God.

If there are things in the mix that make you feel bad, things you've done or said, realise the fact, face up to it, and fix it if you can. If there's stuff that won't go away easily, big stuff that needs attention, talk to someone about it. Talk to God about it. If you need to forgive, do it. If you need to ask forgiveness, do it. Clear the decks, see where you're going in your life, and try to change direction if you can. This is more easily said than done, of course. Prayer and meditation will help, but they will also tend to bring it out into the open. It's important to realise this at the very start.

Once again, don't forget the good stuff. Confession should be as much about that as any failings and shortcomings. Admit the good and bad stuff to God and to yourself. Who and what we are is the sum total of all about us. The truth of us is a mixed up complicated thing, and it lies in the greys as much as the blacks and whites of our lives. All this is how we can get to know and understand the complexity of ourselves, and begin to grow understanding and compassion for other people.

What are meditation and prayer?

Meditation and prayer are names for varieties of mental and physical spiritual practice. They exist more as places on a spectrum than as totally separate things. At the one end is silent, wordless meditation. At the other is petitionary prayer, intercession or conversational prayer. Not everything suits everyone, and most people find styles of prayer and meditation that are a good fit for them personally. At the same time it's worth knowing what's available. Most of us in the churches were only ever taught certain styles of prayer, but there is a lot more out there than the average worshipper ever comes across. At other times in our lives, in different situations, certain prayer styles are more apt. We grow in our faith and in what we need from it as we go along. Even so, the most basic types of prayer, intercession and conversational prayer are ones we should always keep with us. Meditation is not a substitute for them. They are where we start, but we should bring them with us all through our spiritual life.

If you want to go up a mountain spiritually, then you will have to learn to pray. Perhaps as a child you were shown how to do it, but never persevered with it. Many of us dropped out of the habit in our teens, or perhaps never formed a habit in the first place. It takes time, it takes effort, and sometimes it is harder to do than others. If we want to have a relationship with God, there is no other way than to pray. Meditation is a form of prayer, and many kinds of meditation don't even use words. They are silent, using the breath, or movement, or some other object to concentrate on. Obviously some things may be better for doing when up actual mountains than others, but nearly anything is possible anywhere if you put your mind to it!

How to begin?

That depends very much on who you are and where you're coming from. If you have a faith background, perhaps you might be able to resurrect some of the things that are still lurking at the back of your subconscious from before; the conversational prayer or communal prayers that you learned years ago. They may need some updating if you haven't prayed for some time! If those still resonate with you by all means start there. If they no longer have any meaning or sense for you, or you have bad associations with them, start with something new, like one of the other forms of meditation. Walking or breath meditation for instance. Or try just talking to God, one to one, in the silence of your own heart. God is present, God understands. Just talk!

All prayer and meditation techniques involve skills that have to be acquired and learned. Concentration is probably the primary skill, but that comes through time and practice like anything else. Practice is the main thing. Practice and patience with oneself. These are foundational skills to take you through a lifetime. We can't expect spectacular results from a once-off, two-minute trial! We have to give it time. People are recommended to meditate or pray a couple of times a day at least, spending at least fifteen minutes each time to start with. Overdoing it at the beginning can put you off; not giving it enough time will have little outcome. Starting off small and building up over time is probably the best way to go about it. And even one minute is better than no minutes at all!

Spending an afternoon or an entire day mindfully aware as much as possible of God's presence with us, with times spent in varieties of formal prayer or meditation, with gaps between of walking or climbing or some other peaceful activity, can be a refreshing, encouraging way to get some good out of prayer and meditation. A day on the mountain.

What's the point?

What we're trying to do is increase the time we spend with God. Spending time actually talking to God is important, but you can't be at that *all* the time, which is where meditation comes in. After a while, the mental states learned and experienced within meditation can be extended into the rest of our lives. We can develop a 'background awareness' of the presence of God. We also develop a background awareness of ourselves, how we think, how we feel, what's going on inside us. This leads to deep insights into who we actually are in ourselves. Not only that, it gives us deeper insights into other people, who in the end, obviously, aren't that different from us. Deeper insights which lead to stronger compassion and the openness to love other people, as Christ commanded.

Christ's teaching about the kingdom of God was that it was mysterious, but it was here, now, amongst us and available to us. The kingdom, or if you like, the 'Imperial Rule' of God is present to us now in our daily lives. We can live in the same reality that God inhabits, the kingdom. We can live by its rules and customs and expectations, even within and around the rules and expectations of the prevailing culture around us. But doing that requires another way of thinking and perceiving the world and the people in it. Prayer and meditation are the key to growing that thought and perception. Psychologists would say that we are training our minds, taking advantage of neural flexibility to realign neural pathways in the brain and produce new behaviours and establish new patterns of thinking. This is true. Equally truly, in spiritual terms, religious terms, and not in any way contradicting the psychologists, we could say that we are allowing space within ourselves for God, the Holy Spirit, to change and mould us. That isn't done *to* us, it is done with our permission and our welcoming acceptance. We are part of the process, and with help we can grow into new life in God, living in the kingdom, living in true uncon-ditioned reality, not the culturally conditioned dreamworld we usually inhabit.

Belief
Prayer and meditation are what you *have* to do if you're going to be spiritual, religious, and if you say you believe in a God. Prayer means there is a relationship, communication, contact, caring, and attention. Prayer is primary, essential, not just an option for now and again. Just saying that you think there probably is a God doesn't make you either religious or spiritual. It certainly isn't the same as believing in a God. Belief isn't just assenting to the existence of God, ticking a box; it means and implies a relationship. Relationship means that you have to do something about it.

Once upon a time, 'belief' meant trusting. The second part of the word, '-lief', still exists in some English dialects. It comes from the same root as 'love'. It implies personal faith, in the sense of trusting and reliance. The more recent idea of 'belief', meaning that you totally accept something – an idea, a story, a concept – without question, query or quibble, is something that has only come up in the last three hundred years in reaction to the whole scientific enlightenment. Nowadays, too, the word 'faith' equates with the modern idea of believing, but it originally meant fidelity, commitment and trust. Neither word, faith or belief, is to do with thinking something is factually correct, or exists, or happened. They are to do with personal relationship and commitment. Which is how we are to approach the idea of God. This is not about science and proof and certainty. This is personal, with all the meanings of that word at a deep, intuitive and emotional level. We are each personal beings, whether we like that or not. We have no other way to relate to the world, the universe, and God.

Small Doubt and Great Doubt
So to say that you believe in God implicitly invites you to make a further act of trust, to take a chance and find out about that God. It invites you to take a step off a hundred-foot pole, or off a metaphorical cliff, into you know not what. It invites you to come and find out. Doubt is permitted. Doubt is a healthy human reaction to anyone making claims. It keeps us safe in the big wide world, and stops us acquiring dodgy cars and horses with three legs. But sometimes you have to take a chance. This is one of those times. By all means bring your doubts along with you. Test and try, taste and see. You don't have to send all your money anywhere; you aren't signing your life or your house away. Humanity up until our times thought that religion, spirituality was a good thing, and most humans still do. It's built into us. It's still worth taking a look.

There are two kinds of doubt. The first is Small Doubt. Small Doubt tends to make us dismiss things without really trying them and giving them a fair go. That kind of doubt stops us going anywhere or doing anything. The other kind of doubt is Great Doubt and is a sort of wisdom that allows us to sift and judge and measure as we go along, but it allows movement, experiment, trial. This is a good thing to have about you, even in terms of religion. (Perhaps especially in terms of religion!) In the story of the man in the desert with no food or water, he's following a road, and the road forks. He cannot go back, he can only go forwards. If he takes the wrong way he may die; but if he does go on he may discover food and water and help. On the other hand if he stays where he is, just because he isn't sure of the road ahead, he will die for certain anyway. Small Doubt, which stops him moving at all, will kill him. Great Doubt, which allows questioning and exploration, may save his life.

There are varieties of Christianity which say you have to accept unquestioningly first and foremost. I, and others like me, would say you need to trust a bit at the start, and then try and test everything that comes along fairly and kindly, attempting to understand it fully before dismissing or accepting it, and always remembering that your – our – understanding may not be complete.

So, bring your doubt with you, it will keep you sane and help you sort out the good stuff from the rubbish and drivel that floats around the margins of any faith. Or what is necessary from what might not be necessary. Great Doubt, like a sharp sword that cuts nonsense from truth, is a good thing to have about you. On the other hand, the doubt which stops you even trying to find out is deadly. You will always stand on the edge of eternal truth, wondering.

If the package on offer in one place doesn't suit you, isn't making sense, or even worries you, try somewhere else. Read widely, using liberal sprinklings of Great Doubt while you're at it. Seek and look and ask questions. Torment your local cleric, they'll probably welcome the stimulation. If they don't, find one that will. There is much to learn and find out, much to understand and absorb. Don't even trust me, I'm just another eejit walking the road like yourself! As St Paul said, 'Test everything, and hold fast to that which is good.' (1 Thessalonians 5:21) But the one thing common to all faiths is prayer. Prayer is a good place to start, wherever you end up.

Relationship

Belief, in the sense of trusting, implies some sort of a relationship. Religion is not a detached academic pursuit. It involves your very mind and being, and how that comes from and relates to the universe and whatever underlies it. This is why we talk in personal terms. This is you, your very heart and core, connecting to the very heart, core and origin of all that is. The only way humans can handle that sort of stuff is in terms of personal and intimate relationship. This means that you have to *do* something. Merely waving occasionally, as with a distant neighbour, is not enough. This is *personal*. You don't have a relationship with someone you don't know. You can't have a relationship with someone you aren't talking to. You only get to know people, to make the relationship real, through being with them and talking to them and finding out about them. Relationship brings change, if it's a particularly deep one, as in a marriage. Both people in a very close relationship are in a constant process of learning and adjustment and cooperation. That's a working, living relationship. So prayer and/or meditation – conversation, active, living relationship – is obligatory. And it will change you.

Types of Prayer

1. Conversational Prayer

When we pray, we talk to God. It's that simple. Conversational prayer is the most basic form of prayer, and sometimes the most moving and effective. You just freely talk to God. God knows and understands you totally and is closer to you than you are to yourself, and is accepting and loving and completely comprehends where you're coming from and why you are where you are. You can let it all out, be thankful, sad, angry, totally pissed off, happy – whatever state you are in. Talking about it helps, as they say. Being with someone who cares and understands helps.

Don't expect 'spoken' conversational answers, by the way. The voices in your head are your own mind. Your mind will supply answers to anything you ask, and pretend to be someone else if you really want it to. It will come up with challenging answers or comforting answers, but you are still only talking to yourself. Your mind is a very complicated thing, and do not trust it. Great Doubt is necessary. When God answers, he is extremely unlikely to do it in a conversational reply; God will do it in his own way, in his own time. All prayer is heard, but God doesn't, regularly, in the ordinary normal course of events, have conversations with people. Let's be serious here. Be wary of people who say, 'God talks to me.'

Notice, that when we talk to God we personalise him. We call him 'him' for a start, though calling him 'her' will cause no offence nor make any difference. Use whatever pronoun suits you. Neither is the truth. Personalising God is a natural human thing to do. We only know how to talk to people, we don't know how to talk to anything else. So we talk to God as a person. That's fair enough, and continuing to do that is fine. We just need to keep in mind that none of the ideas and concepts we have of God, the images and pictures, are the whole story. They are only part of the story. God is pretty incomprehensible. God doesn't actually fit under any of the terms or ideas we have for things or people in our ordinary life: a person, or entity, or being, or even concept. But we talk to God as if he was our father or grandfather, or our mother; that's how humans work, we can do no different. Using temporary images of God in our minds is a natural, necessary thing to do.

In times past, people thought of and talked to God as if he was a high lord, a great king; people with the power of life and death over you existed in their worlds. That way of thinking pushes God too far away from us, making him distant and strange. Most of us don't have people we think of in quite that way any more, thankfully enough, so terms like that don't work for us very well. The Lord, or even THE LORD has become another name for God, rather than something that means anything much. Then again, at the other extreme, we can allow God to become too much our personal cuddly friend, when in fact we are communicating with the whatever-it-is beyond our understanding that came up with existence in the first place. Keeping the balance in how we think of God is important, perhaps in different ways at different times.

Jesus for most Christians is synonymous with God, or the same as God. (Yes, I know about the Trinity, but this is how people think.) When they pray to Jesus they're talking to God. You can also, of course, talk to God directly, but the usual way of doing that is by finishing off with Christ's name, 'through Christ Our Lord' or 'for the sake of your Son, Jesus Christ' or a variant of that. Jesus is the human face of God, the recognisable face that we can relate to and talk to and understand, because he was and is a human person. Many Christians believe that they can only approach God through Christ, since God is perceived as being too high up and too far removed for the likes of us to speak to him, part of the 'High-Lord-God-Almighty' way of thinking. That wasn't exactly what Christ taught. He called God 'Abba' – 'Daddy' – and encouraged his followers to pray to God themselves. How you do it is up to yourself, though different churches would have varying emphases. I don't think God worries too much as long as we're talking at all!

2. Communal Prayer

One step away from conversational prayer is the use of pre-existing forms of prayer, like the Lord's Prayer, or the communal forms of prayer we would use in services in a church. Those are good. Many of them have deep teaching within them, attitudes and ways of thinking worth learning and considering. They are a digestible way of acquiring theological thoughts, and are usually easily remembered.

Actually taking part in prayer with other people in community is also important. Coming together regularly as a group is something all religions do, and for very good reasons. At the very least, many people feel they get much more from prayer and meditation when they do them together with others. It also encourages us towards having a regular prayer life on our own behalf, and can inform, strengthen and freshen our faith and practice.

Communal prayer is central to faith, to religion. We do not exist as individuals, separate from everyone else. We exist only as part of other people. It was other people who brought us up, minded us, made sure we were fed and washed and cared for. It is other people we work with, depend on still for help and care when we need it. Being independent is seen as being a virtue in our present society. Most of us have the money to be able to afford to pay for the privilege. But we are only fooling ourselves, putting a barrier between us and other people, buying a privacy that is only an expensive, temporary isolation. That is not good for us. We are societal, communal, family animals. We are designed to be part of a group, and that keeps us healthy and well adjusted and safe in ourselves. This is also true in a spiritual sense. To be a solitary hermit is something only for very few indeed. A little solitude is a good thing for all of us, but being together with others, to pray, worship, discuss, learn – to live – is what it's all about.

If you're going to explore faith, then being a member of a worshipping community is a good idea. It keeps you in contact with the living tradition that has come down through many generations. Being with a group of other people also means that we can become exposed to a healthy breadth of faith, opinion, and approach. On our own we can wander off the map and end up with a faith which fits our own wishes and needs too exactly without challenging them. The nice bits and the prickly bits are all necessary! At the same time, there are different approaches in different churches and denominations, and opinions differ even between one cleric, parish or congregation and another in the same outfit. This is not usually said out loud in religious circles – it can pay to shop around. But do remember that what you don't like may sometimes be good for you!

3. Psalms

The Psalms are a book of ancient hymns, poems and prayers (and curses!) in the Old Testament. We can also use the psalms to pray. That was the tradition in monasteries from the very beginning, using the Psalter for their daily prayer cycle. It takes a bit of thinking and getting used to, to be honest, but it's still the basis of the Daily Office, which is worth taking a look at. Both the Roman Catholic and Anglican churches have versions of it, and while it is designed for priests and monastics, many lay people use it as well. It's a collection of psalms, prayers and intercessions for use at different times during the day. There are simplified forms available, or huge three volume sets. (See the Booklist for examples.) You can pray it on your own and still realise that you are praying together with many thousands of other people all doing the same thing elsewhere in the world. The Daily Office is a way of 'sanctifying' time, of bringing our minds and hearts back again and again to God as we go through the day. Used over time, like any spiritual practice, it begins to mould our thoughts and minds in new ways. The psalms are still very human and accessible, even if some of them are perhaps almost three thousand years old. People are still people.

4. Prayer of Intercession

Intercession, praying for ourselves or other people, tends to make up the largest chunk of verbal prayer, though usage may vary, as they say. Asking God for things in our own lives, or for other people, whether those close to us or far away, is a good thing to do. Will it make a difference? That's not our business, that's God's business. It still definitely does us good. It changes us, makes us more generous and compassionate, makes us aware of the state of the world, gives us perspective into ourselves and how we think and how well off we are already. Prayer changes us in good ways we don't expect or plan for.

When we pray deeply and sincerely for healing for someone we know, for example, we are taking that person and their situation deep into ourselves. We are allowing them and their pain to become part of our awareness, we are giving it attention, and attention is the backbone of love. Not sentiment or 'feeling nice' but paying considerate attention to people's requirements, to their feelings, to their ongoing experience. This is the nub and core of love and compassion, the bit that will get us up off our backsides and get us out there doing something for someone. Prayer can and will nurture that within us. Then we can go out and make things happen, change things, even as we are changed. This is where we should be concentrating, not on what God's doing. God's doing what he's supposed to be doing. We can and must share our world with God, our concerns and worries, and the concerns and worries of those people we come across in our lives, our neighbours.

> The Lord is near. Do not worry about anything, but in everything by prayer and supplication with thanksgiving let your requests be made known to God. And the peace of God, which surpasses all understanding, will guard your hearts and your minds in Christ Jesus.
>
> (*Philippians 4*)

It does need to be said, though, that intercession, or any other form of prayer (or a pilgrimage!) shouldn't be done merely to expect something from it in automatic exchange, a mechanical relationship something like bribing Santa. That would be a form of magic, and magic is us trying to manipulate reality to suit us. Much of the suffering we experience comes from us demanding that the cosmos, reality, be some other way. Our minds are slippery enough to play these games with us, steering us one way and another, trying to find a chink in the universe's armour, to press the right button that will make it work in our favour.

A common fall back position in serious illness, tragedy or bereavement and even in other less serious situations is to try to bargain with God, wheedling, making promises of behavioural change, or money. We try to use our wills, our wiles, to have things changed for us, to exert an influence. It's natural and normal. It's part of our psychology as human beings. God understands our needs, our fears, our grief and our greed all at the same time. God cares, God pays attention.

In the prayer our Lord gave us, the fourth phrase is: 'Thy will be done.' This is the key to intercession. It is no sin to bring a trouble to God, no sin to ask him to fix it. It is a good thing, it is sharing a trouble with a friend, it is confirming a relationship, affirming trust. Where we go astray is when we seek to deny reality, condemn it for being what it is, and demand Special Treatment. What Christ teaches is: 'Your Father in heaven … makes his sun rise on the evil and on the good, and sends rain on the righteous and on the unrighteous' (Matthew 19). God is not fair, God is love. Love is not fair, love just loves. Unconditional love like that isn't logical, isn't preferential, and doesn't make sense. Part of spiritual maturity is us beginning to understand that, and to begin to glimpse what 'the will of God' is. We must constantly remember that we are not living in a Harry Potter film or a novel. We are where we are, here and now in this place, this body, this frame of mind, this culture, this personal situation. Where spirituality and its practices can take us is to acceptance and understanding and patience and strength and compassion for others and for ourselves. They can allow us to see the imaginary, fantasy world we create to live in, and assist us in finding the real world. They leave us in a better place, and in a better relationship with God.

Miracles are always, only, a last resort and an outside chance. There are no foolproof, fail-safe forms of prayer that will get you exactly what you want from God (or any other celestial being for that matter) when you want it. Even if you do it nine times, and publish it in a newspaper. God doesn't work like that, God is not an eejit, he has more sense than we do. Not everything demanded is given, not everything wished for is granted. Those who do not deserve may receive, and those who are obviously most deserving may go without. It is not simple, not magic. But one thing is true, whatever is received or not, given or not, granted or not, we are the better for having prayed, for having asked, for having spent the time in God's presence. We are the better for having shown our love to God; or if we aren't up to that, we are better even for the respect, the acknowledgment of God's presence and existence and attention to us. The asking itself is about relationship, about revealing to ourselves, even if God knows already, what we need or want. We're allowed to ask for ourselves as well as other people: we are to love our neighbour as ourselves – and vice versa. We are in there too. Cutting ourselves out is false modesty and flawed humility, which is harmful rather than laudable.

God has no needs. We have nothing to offer him. But we can share with God, understand, cooperate, make real God's existence for ourselves, and, more than that, understand our own existence and relation to all that is around us. In God, through God, we can have a meaningful relationship with ourselves and others, rather than blindly existing in a cultural dream game. In the kingdom of God, the stance we have to take is one of open trust. Trust that I am cared for, cared about, as are we all. This is not a matter of total fatalistic passivity in the face of whatever life turns up. We're allowed to talk about it or give out about it, and we'd be strange if we didn't! But trusting love gives calmness and clears away the nonsense and panic. It allows one to act, gives the space to see clearly what the right thing is to do, without fear or mindless conditioned reaction, or the mixed motives or agendas one has hidden even from oneself. Prayer in the kingdom, modelled on Christ's own prayer (the Lord's Prayer), is one based on a realistic, open-eyed relationship to the whole of existence. It takes into consideration our own nature and needs, and also the reality of being. In this lies the 'Peace of God which passes all understanding', the peace Christ promised us.

5. Lectio Divina

A central spiritual activity of most faiths who have a sacred book, or scripture, is reading it in a spiritual way, rather than just for information or study. In the Christian tradition that is known as Lectio Divina, 'holy reading'.

Scripture is funny stuff. It's not the same as other books – textbooks or novels or newspapers. People have been reading it over and over for perhaps thousands of years. They think of it in a distinct way from everything else. It has become 'holy', and 'sacred' which again means set apart, special. Some people, Moslems, and some Christians, say their scripture consists of actual words coming directly from God, breathed (inspired) by God into the author. Other Christians say that the Bible might be inspired by God, but in the more usual sense of that word in our world. It is special: it is people's thinking and talking and discussion and understanding of God and things to do with God. It points towards God, but it isn't necessarily God's actual voice written down.

Scripture is complicated stuff. Even the most recent bits of the Bible are nearly two thousand years old, and the oldest are well over three thousand years old, written in ancient languages, cultures and contexts. So it's not that easy to understand, necessarily. Sections of it may only be of interest to a scholar; parts of it are very moving and important. There's poetry, history, stories, laws, advice, prophecy and on and on. It's a library in itself, so you can't take it all the same way. The Buddha said that scripture was like a snake, you have to know the right way to pick it up, or it will turn around and bite you. You have to be careful. So it may not always say what you think it says, or would like it to say. It may be very simple and straightforward or it may not. It may say something over here, and something entirely contradictory over there. There are books to explain stuff, to help you read your way through the texts, and those are worth looking at to help you make sense of what's going on. But, in the end, you have to sit down with the writing on the page and read it. Just you and it, and God. That's when Lectio Divina can happen.

Choose a short passage, just a few verses. Compose yourself in a quiet place, ask God to quieten your heart and mind. After a few moments, when you feel ready, begin to read. There are four parts to the process of Lectio Divina:

Lectio (reading): Read the passage slowly, prayerfully, pausing at the end of lines or sentences or phrases, perhaps reading aloud.

Meditatio (reflecting): Read the passage again, and allow yourself to become aware of a phrase or group of words or just one word that stands out for you. What floats to the surface of the reading? Spend time with the phrase. 'Chew' it mentally for a while. Take it into yourself. What is the meaning of it, on the surface, or deep within it, or in relation to your own life or circumstances? Don't expect mind-blowing revelations or weird stuff to happen. This is about being in God's presence at a deep, quiet level.

Oratio (prayer/response): Speak to God, in words or images or feelings. Interact with him the same way you would with someone who knows you deeply and intimately. What insights are in this word or phrase for you?

Contemplatio (resting): Rest in God's presence with you, in silence and peace for a moment. When you feel like returning to prayer or reading do so, but take your time.

All this is not something to be rushed, and it is a skill to be learned. That takes time and practice and patience. There will always be good days and bad days.

Lectio Divina is possibly most rewarding done with texts from the gospels, or perhaps the Psalms. We can actually sense the voice of Christ, for instance, speaking to us through the text, and in the right circumstances it can have great depth and impact and meaning for us. Far above and beyond simply hearing it read out in a church or a cursory reading of our own. This is a much more personal thing, a communication between us and God. That said, there are good reasons to do this in the company of other people or even at least with the advice of a commentary beside us, so that we are informed and nurtured and helped to grow by a faith community.

(NB: Not everybody in religious goings on, even in the same church, agrees with everybody else, in case you haven't noticed. That's ok. Nothing strange there. People don't agree about politics either, and scientists bicker amongst themselves too. That's people. Get used to it, but keep your reason and sense about you – Great Doubt – at all times! And be nice to other people whatever happens!)

6. Ignation Meditation

Ignatian meditation is another way of using scripture in prayer. Here, we pick a passage, usually from the gospels, and, having read it slowly a couple of times, we bring the scene to life within our imaginations. We actually become a participant, or at least a close spectator at the various episodes in the gospel story. We can interact with Christ himself, ask questions, talk to him. This can be a very successful form of prayer, very intimate, giving us insights in a way simply talking won't achieve. It's the form of prayer espoused by the Jesuit Order and widely taught by them. You can do it as part of a group where someone talks you through the story, or on your own.

If you're interested you can find out more on the *Ignatian Spirituality* website, where spiritual exercises can be found (http://www.ignatianspirituality.com/ignatian-prayer/the-spiritual-exercises/).

Simple instructions of how to go about Ignation Mediation:
Find a quiet place and compose yourself. Pray for a while, or
do another form of meditation for a few moments. Talk to God
about what you're about to do and ask him to guide you.
Slowly read a passage from scripture – gospel stories are best.
Perhaps read it a couple of times to get the feel of it. What
stands out for you in it? Now do what you used to do when
you were a child. Imagine you were there, part of it. You can
be a main character or a bystander. Create the scene: the
weather, your clothes, smells, sounds, buildings. Look at
what's going on around you, and who else is there. Who are
they? Now interact with the story, the surroundings. Let
yourself flow into it. Allow yourself to be guided by the Spirit
as you talk to other people. Don't try to take control, let
yourself go along with it. Trust that God is with you. How
does it make you feel in yourself?

As you come to the end, talk to God about what happened,
what it was like, how it affected you. Do you understand now
at a new level? Have you received insights? Is there a depth
to the story you hadn't appreciated before?

Those are the usual forms of verbal prayer most people are
familiar with: conversational and communal prayer, intercession, and prayerful reading of scripture. If you've never
tried any of them before, you'll find they all involve the
acquisition of a level of certain skills we may not have picked
up much of in ordinary life. Skills of concentration and
patience, trust and discipline. Those take time to acquire and
learn, and everyone has good days and bad days, or 'dry'
periods, where the whole thing seems pointless. Perseverance
and patience and compassion for oneself is what gets us over
the humps, or out of the ruts. While it may seem that nothing

is happening in the more uneventful periods of prayer we may pass through, there's more going on than we realise. We are doing work while we pray; we are training ourselves, our hearts and minds. We are exposing ourselves to God, establishing relationship, being changed. The course of our life, of our habits of thought, perception and behaviour are all being deflected from the path they were on before we started. This new direction takes trust, time and effort and, please notice, nobody mentioned the word 'easy' anywhere. You have to put yourself, wholly, completely and generously into it. Here are two famous answers to the question 'how should I pray or meditate?'

> 'Say the prayer as if you were going to die
>   at the end of it.'
>
> > (*The Cloud of Unknowing,
> > fourteenth century, England*)

> 'Like your hair was on fire.'
>
> > (*Eihei Dogen,
> > twelfth century, Japan*)

CHAPTER SEVEN

Meditation

Meditation is a form of prayer, either totally without words, using the breath or movement, or else the words are used as an object to centre and concentrate the mind, rather than for what they specifically mean in themselves. A mantra for example is a short prayer, phrase or word constantly repeated and used as a centre of concentration to keep the mind in one place rather than running around talking to itself, while we spend time in God's company. It's common in Hinduism and Buddhism, and other faiths, but is also found in Christianity in a few forms. Meditation isn't about verbal conversation, it's about just being with God, in his presence. Recognising that he is there, close, with us, around us and in us, not just when we're turning our attention to him, but always. Meditation is the way most people ascend to the higher slopes of the mountain.

The Point of Meditation

There are two sides to this. Christian meditation is trad-itionally directed towards God. God is the point of it, moving closer to God, seeking for oneness, union with God, whatever that might mean. The downside is that the only tool we have to work with is us! Ourselves, our physical body and mind. One thing can't happen without the other. This movement towards God requires preparation and work and effort. The preparation and work is with ourselves, with how we think, who we are, our lives and emotions and feelings, our drives and dislikes and desires. Whether we like it or not, these are going to feature anyway.

One way to think of meditation is allowing a process of 'purification' within us, where we, through and with God, begin to work with all that is in us that isn't pointing in the right direction, the pulls and pushes we constantly receive from our subconscious mind and physicality, needs, urges, dislikes and fears. Once again, you can see this as retraining your mind in a psychological sense, or else allowing the presence of God, the Holy Spirit within you, to work on you, to fit you for the kingdom.

Sit down in utter silence, close your eyes, and what you come across inside your own head is yourself! God is surely present, but what you will actually experience is your thoughts, your itches and pains and sensations, your notions and impulses. On and on and on, as has been happening since you were born. You've spent a lifetime talking to yourself, thinking and fantasising and having urges and needs over and over and over. Whatever notions we might have about inner silence and peace, the racket doesn't stop overnight just because we want or expect it to, or at all, actually! We are born with who we are, and we need to learn to live with that person and understand them. That person is the only individual in the whole world that we have any influence over, and you'll find out pretty quick that she/he doesn't pay much heed to you!

It takes training and practice and time to begin to perceive and untangle the unconscious habits of our entire lives before this. That's what meditation does. It helps us quieten the internal noise so that we can hear the silence of the reality beyond our chatter. That can only happen when we understand and accept ourselves as we are, as God does. It can only happen when we spend time with God, allowing the Holy Spirit to act on us, to train and retrain our minds to see and think differently.

What is the training and concentration for?
Other faiths would have other ideas, of course, but Christians might say it's the way to learn to live in the kingdom of God. God's kingdom doesn't run on the same rules and lines as everywhere else. In all the places humans live there's a thing called culture. That's a sort of agreed way of how to live and get on. It covers houses and languages, clothes and food and manners, politics, law, religion and customs and also how we see and interpret the world around us, and how we get on with other people in it. We're all born into a culture, and we all follow the rules of one culture or another. We don't even know we're doing it. Humans love playing games, and following rules, and culture is a sort of mega-game that everybody plays, and it's very deeply ingrained into us. We all know the rules without thinking about it; we pick them up as we go through childhood.

What Jesus taught, in a way, was that culture wasn't necessarily the best game to run your life by. There is another set of rules, a superior game going on, and that's what we call the kingdom of God. Jesus demonstrates the set of rules for being in it, for playing God's game. God's game is really the only game in town; everything else is just 'let's pretend'. To be honest, what God is doing isn't actually a game at all, it's reality. When we waken up to the fact that we're living in a game that we collectively make up as we go along, it can come as a surprise, but more than one world faith has said as much before now.

Money is a good example of what I mean. Money doesn't really exist, it's just pieces of metal, or bits of paper, or even more weirdly, numbers in a computer. Humans agree to play a game together where this stuff is very important. People die for it or kill for it, and starve because they haven't any, or lose their jobs and livelihoods if the banks and computers get it wrong. Again. Its value can go up or down arbitrarily if someone somewhere decides to change the rules, or if someone cheats. But it doesn't really exist. It's just a game we agree to play together as humans. We made it up.

In the kingdom, there's just reality. There's no money for a start. Value is about real things, about stuff that's actually important: loving and caring for people, minding the environment, being kind, honesty, that kind of stuff. Somewhere in the back of all our heads we already know what's really important, but we forget, and keep playing the game where power, fame, money and good looks are crucial, and other stuff doesn't matter.

God's kingdom is upside down compared to the ordinary world. It points in a different direction, spins on a different axis. Meditation (prayer) helps us reset our mental compasses, change the rules we play by, realise what's actually there, and what we only pretend is there. Or we could say it tunes us into another wavelength, the one that God's on, the one that Christ directs us towards. Meditation and prayer help us create a bit of space in the game we're playing, they let us step outside the game for a while and watch it so that we can see what's really happening. It opens up gaps to let the light in. It gives us glimpses of reality. And reality is where God is.

Methods of Meditation
For all these methods of meditation, it's worth setting a timer. Either a clock, or on your phone. There are a number of meditation apps available. Start low, perhaps 10–15 minutes at first, and build up to a regular period of at least 20 minutes, but up to 30 or 40 minutes, preferably twice a day. But remember, even one minute is better than no minutes. You can do lots of very short meditations throughout the day as well. Just the length of a few breaths in God's presence.

All forms of prayer and meditation share the same problems of concentration and distraction. These are discussed briefly at the end of the chapter.

1. The Jesus Prayer
This is the recitation of the words:

'Lord Jesus Christ, Son of the Living God, have mercy on me, a sinner.'

Or shorter variants of it:

'Lord Jesus Christ, have mercy on me, a sinner.'

'Jesus Christ, have mercy on me.'

'Christ, have mercy.'

It is associated most strongly with the Eastern Orthodox Churches. The technique is to sit quietly, upright, with your eyes closed or open, and say the words mentally in time with your in-breath and out-breath. Perhaps for ten minutes or so at first. Keep your mind gently concentrated on the words, in time with your breathing, and when it wanders off, as it surely will, bring it gently back to the words again. We are told to say it within our heart. After a while (and this means a *very* long while, by the way), they say the heart begins to recite the prayer itself, so natural has it become. This way our minds can pray constantly while we go about our business!

The line itself isn't as penitential as it first appears. For most people, asking for mercy really means 'please don't hit me again'. This is not what we're doing. Mercy may have this meaning, but it also has the meaning of favour, goodness, and compassion. Much more positive attributes. Unfortunately, the 'sinner' bit is probably true, though as we can all be considered equally as sinners it may not mean as much as you think. Best, perhaps, to understand it in terms of honest humility. Humility isn't about saying (and convincing yourself) that you are the lowest of the low. It *is* about realising what you really are, being realistic about yourself, perceptive about your true nature in its totality. Not judging or comparing or condemning, just being honestly transparent to yourself. God sees us all with the same loving eye. We need to learn that trick too.

The Jesus Prayer comes from an urge to be constantly and consciously in God's presence. To pray always, as St Paul says, 'Pray in the Spirit at all times in every prayer and supplication' (Ephesians 9); 'Rejoice always, pray without ceasing, give thanks in all circumstances; for this is the will of God in Christ Jesus for you' (1 Thessalonians 16–18). Early monastics took this line about unceasing prayer seriously. In the first centuries of Christianity they went out to the desert and lived in scattered communities, and these Desert Fathers (and Mothers) were the first recorded as being Christian meditators. (See Booklist.)

To be perfectly honest, although the words of the Jesus Prayer are hallowed by time, tradition and usage, and that's worth paying heed to, the words themselves are secondary. Cassian for instance, in the fourth century, tells us the Desert Fathers used: 'O Lord make speed to save us. O God make haste to help us' (Psalm 40) as a mantra. We could just say the word 'Jesus' or 'Love' or something apt. It would work the same way. Our intention, the direction of our meditation is the main thing. The method Dom John Main taught, Christian meditation (featured below), uses the word 'Maranatha'.

2. The Rosary

This is very widely known, though it is quite a complicated form of mental prayer. It was developed in the middle ages, as a poor person's form of the Monastic Offices. Saying the Office required one to be literate, and only a few people were. But the rest were well able to recite prayers that they had learned by rote: the Hail Mary, the Our Father, the Gloria and the Creed. All of which go to make up a recitation of the Rosary, simultaneously combined with recollections of scriptural episodes in Jesus' life.

I don't give detailed instructions for it here because they're quite easily accessible elsewhere on many, many websites. If you were born into the Roman Catholic tradition you probably have at least a nodding acquaintance with it. If you are already familiar with it, it might be a good place to begin. If it isn't a part of your own spiritual tradition, there are such things as Protestant forms of the Rosary, which you could find on the internet if you were interested. But all in all the Rosary is a complex, many-layered form of meditation which would take some time to learn and become proficient in if you weren't brought up with it. There are easier places to start, though you might like to come back to it when you've got used to meditation and prayer and would like to have a go.

Beads

The Rosary and the Jesus Prayer are traditionally said on beads. The word 'bead' (*bede*) means a prayer. Another common neutral spiritual technology. Buddhism, Hinduism and Islam also use a rosary, or *mala* (a garland). In the Orthodox Churches, a prayer rope or *chotke*, a knotted string or small rope, is used to keep the count. All these act as primitive, pre-clockwork timers, as well as counters. They come in different lengths, from 10 or 25 beads, up to 100 or more, or 108 beads on a *mala*. Being aware of the feel of the beads on your fingers, plus the mantra, is a good concentration object. All rosaries, *malas* or *chotki* are considered as being 'special' objects, not for ordinary decoration of the person, very personal, and for prayer use only.

In the end, the number of recitations isn't important; it's the amount of time spent in God's company, and how we spend that time. There isn't a competition, and no one is keeping score.

3. Christian Meditation and Centering Prayer

Another style of mantra meditation is that known as Christian Meditation as propagated by John Main, a Benedictine monk. The website of the World Community for Christian meditation (www.wccm.org) is worth looking at and their publications are also worth perusing. This form of meditation is closely related to Centering Prayer as propagated by Fr Thomas Keating (www.contemplativeoutreach.org). Look at them both to see which might suit you best.

Christian Meditation is centred around physical stillness and internal repetition of the mantra (or prayer-word) 'Maranatha', stressing each syllable equally (Ma-ra-na-tha). This prayer-word is used to anchor your mind and dispel any distractions. Detailed instructions are found on the World Community for Christian Meditation website, where it is recommended that one should meditate for thirty minutes each morning and evening.

Centering Prayer also involves the use of a sacred word (of your choosing) as 'the symbol of your intention to consent to God's presence and action within'. Again, in physical stillness, with eyes closed, and remaining in silence, this sacred word is used to anchor your thoughts for the prayer period. Guidelines for practising Centering Prayer are available on the Contemplative Outreach website.

Silent Meditation

Some meditation techniques don't involve any words at all. Instead of a mantra, we use something else on which to centre our awareness. Some people feel uncomfortable not using something obviously and explicitly religious as part of a meditation, but if we really believe that God is there, with us, and we in him, then what's the problem? We are just in communication with God in another way. Good friends and old married couples don't always have to talk, they can just be content in each other's company. It's a matter of trust. So too with God. God knows, so do we. Talking isn't always required. We can just *be* with God. Indeed 'being religious' can sometimes miss the point and get in the way. Just being, just allowing ourselves to be, can be a deeply spiritual and religious act.

At the same time, I don't recommend silent meditation as a total replacement for intercessory prayer. That is still a good thing to do, and is irreplaceable in the way that it opens us up to the world outside ourselves and feeds our compassion and generosity. Conversational prayer as well is still a worthwhile thing to keep on. We are very complex animals, and sometimes talking is the only thing that works for us, and can allow the various sides and parts of us to make themselves known.

Here below are instructions for four types of meditation: breathing meditation, walking meditation, a body scan, and lovingkindness meditation. The first three can be used as a basic formal everyday meditation practice. The fourth is to teach ourselves a more specific skill. These techniques are borrowed (shamelessly) from the Buddhists, who have spent more time than possibly any other faith in researching this neutral spiritual technology. They are worth listening to when they talk about meditation, and they have much to teach Christians, I believe. The Buddhists are far ahead of the field in the study of meditation, especially with the idea of mental training to make us fit for purpose in ourselves: more loving, caring and open. This is the reason that Christians would wish to use it in their everyday lives. This kind of meditation is practical, useful and effective. It can teach us how to be better Christians. Meditation has been viewed with some doubt in Christian circles, or seen as reserved for monastics, or a small spiritual elite. In fact it can be a fulfilling part of anyone's spiritual life, and, even if only done at a basic level, is a great source of spiritual insight, as well as a practical help in day-to-day life and relationships.

Some people are confused about how you would pray without words. You do it by just sitting. Just being there with God. It feels like there's just you and just God – and traffic noise and phones and itches and pains in your back and your knees and thinking and more thinking and tunes and songs passing through your brain, and remembering stuff, and replaying the fight you had last week with a colleague in work and worries about your children, or your job, or what's happening next week, and the shopping and on and on and on. You keep bringing your attention back to your word, or your breath or whatever you're using as an anchor to stop you getting lost in your own mind. Over and over again. After a while you get better at it. It quietens down a bit. It's peaceful some days, noisier others. But God is always there. The point of our meditation, our intention in it is simply being with God.

What it teaches you most in the beginning, is about you, primarily. About your place in the world, about how you think, about who you are, and why you are the way you are. It teaches you about what's important and what's not. We begin to see ourselves in a new light. Spending time with someone else means they rub off on you. Spend time with God and a lot rubs off on you. God knows it all already. God is always there. God loves and accepts you. In his company you don't need any masks and pretence. There's just you and God. In God and with God and through God we derive insight and wisdom and depth. We learn to love and have compassion for ourselves and for other people.

Meditation is a catch-all term for many techniques and ideas. It can too often be perceived and promoted as a very wobbly, soft, warm and comforting idea. A nice relaxing form of prayer. In truth, this is *not* most people's experience of it. It is simple but hard, sometimes very difficult. But it works. It changes things. It does things. Physically, neurally, it affects our minds and bodies. As a result it is recommended in the medical world for chronic pain, blood-pressure, stress and some other ailments; it is increasingly used in cognitive behavioural therapy and in some cases of depression. Meditation has a real effect, it is not some kind of mystical, spiritual mumbo jumbo. (Though it can be – keep Great Doubt handy at all times!)

As a neutral technique for training the mind, meditation can be used to improve ourselves at any activity we do: sport,

121

writing, playing poker, music, washing dishes, even to learn to become better at killing people. We are using it to become better Christians.

Spiritually speaking, meditation can take you places you would not ordinarily go. The mystical tradition, as seen in St John of the Cross and Teresa of Avila, Cassian, the Desert Fathers, the Fathers quoted in the Philokalia, the writer of the *Cloud of Unknowing* and others like Tony De Mello and Thomas Merton (see Booklist), traces that path in Christianity. If it suits you, it is a good path to follow, but perhaps not everyone is called to it. Just reading this book will introduce you to the lower slopes of spiritual meditative practice as a way of starting to climb the mountain; anyone can do it, young or old, whether they feel themselves to be deeply spiritual or not. The breathing meditation technique may take you to the very top of the mountain if you wish to go, but it will teach you more than is sufficient for life in the valleys as well. The techniques are simple enough for children to have a go at, and as a life-long habit and practice, will change you. Whether that is a matter of neural plasticity, or our disposing ourselves to receive the grace of God really doesn't matter, both things are simultaneously true, and worth remembering.

Preliminaries

The basic instructions below are useful in any of the sitting meditations here.

I open all my meditations with: 'In the name of the Father, and of the Son and of the Holy Spirit.'I then say the prayer 'The Collect for Purity', used as the first words of the famous fourteenth century English book on meditation, *The Cloud of Unknowing*, and also at the beginning of the Eucharist in the Anglican tradition.

The Collect for Purity
Almighty God,
to whom all hearts are open,
all desires known,
and from whom no secrets are hidden;
Cleanse the thoughts of our hearts,
by the inspiration of your Holy Spirit,
that we may perfectly love you,
and worthily magnify your holy name;
through Christ our Lord. Amen.

(Book of Common Prayer)

I would usually say a prayer of thanks at the end, or the Our Father, and perhaps a brief lovingkindness meditation (see below). You are of course free to work out your own introductory process. Ritual helps our minds to get into a certain way of thinking. On finishing any meditation, don't just get up and walk away, become aware of how you feel, and try to take the mindful attention and awareness with you when you go. It is important that the mindset experienced in meditation, or aimed at, at least, is brought into our whole lives and not just reserved for formal periods of 'being religious'. Awareness of the presence of God, insofar as we are able; awareness of our feelings and sensations; unjudgemental awareness of those around us, of our and their behaviour and speech, and of the emotions we experience; all this goes to make up our total experience of reality. Perhaps only glimpses are possible at first, but this is what we are aiming for.

Sit with dignity. Posture is very important. Sitting correctly will affect your mental state, even your mood, positively. Slump and lean, and you will doze and mentally wander all the more. It is best to sit on the very edge of a chair, keeping your back straight, head up. Put your hands on your thighs, or together on your lap. Keep your feet flat on the floor. A cushion under the base of the spine when sitting on a chair can help with posture. You can sit on the floor if you feel that suits, with a cushion to keep your back straight and with legs crossed. There are various poses you can use, from the Lotus, Half Lotus, or just crossed legs, whichever your anatomy is capable of! You may also kneel, and a small bench is helpful here. Being dignified but relaxed is the main thing.

Try not to move. Whether you are sitting on a chair, or on the floor, pains and aches will probably arise at some stage. If you must readjust your position for any reason, try to do so gently and mindfully.

Take the space of a few breaths to centre yourself: feel the tone of your body, relax any tension, become aware of any pains or sensations, then let them go; become aware of the sounds around you for a few breaths, then let them go as well. One helpful image is of something sinking slowly into deeper and deeper water.

Eyes shut, or half opened, or fully opened, it's up to you. If open, keep them gently unfocussed on a spot a few feet in front of you. Closed eyes may make you more liable to go to sleep. Breathe through your nose, keep your tongue behind your upper teeth, jaws not clenched, mouth closed. Face relaxed.

1. Basic Breathing Meditation

Focus attention on your breath. Where do you feel it most? Traditionally you're advised to concentrate on it at the nose, or at the base of the abdomen just below your navel. Just feel it going in or out, or the belly rising and falling. Don't tamper with it, just feel it and keep your attention on the same place.

When the mind wanders, which it surely will, just lightly, silently, label what was going on – dreaming, thinking, feeling, seeing, listening, whatever it was – and gently bring the attention back to the breath. You will do this millions of times. Eventually your mind will begin to quieten down. Or the gaps between thoughts will widen, however you like to think of it. Don't force it, just follow the breath. Be aware of the whole breath, the gaps between inhalation and exhalation, the length of it, the nature and texture of it. Be interested in the breath, the kind of it. Don't force yourself. Play with the experience. Let it be interesting and fun, as far as possible.

As aids to keep concentration in the first while you can:

Simply say mentally 'in' and 'out' with each breath.

Or

Count up to ten breaths, beginning at 'one' again each time. Each inhalation and exhalation together counting as one breath. Mentally say, 'one' for an inhalation, again for an exhalation, and so forth. 'Two' for the next inhalation, etc.

Or

When you are able to regularly keep your concentration for ten full breaths, then try counting up to ten, and back down to one. When you are able to keep your concentration for a few decades, you may drop the counting and simply follow the breath.

Once you are able to concentrate to some extent (and that might take some time!) bring mindfulness into play. Use the breath as an anchor: whatever arises in consciousness, pay attention to it for a few breaths, and then return to the breathing. Label it briefly and lightly, thinking: a pain, a sensation, a noise, a mental image, whatever it is. Become aware of the workings of your own interior self, but don't get caught up in them. Use the breath to anchor your attention.

There are two layers to meditation:

1. Watching the breath, and following it intently, teaches peace, concentration, and it quietens the mind. Concentration is an important ingredient, but on its own it can be empty.

2. Built on that, but not separable from it, is awareness or mindfulness: watching, seeing what comes up. Without concentration, this is not possible because we will be sucked into our own thoughts and notions again. But to sit and become aware of thought, emotion and sensation is a very significant part of the whole thing. Most importantly, this should happen not only in formal meditation but in the rest of life. It will naturally spill out into how we live, and should be encouraged to do so. This awareness leaves space for God, for change, for the growth of compassion, wisdom, love.

Please notice that you aren't trying to stop thinking, that's impossible, but you will be enabled to be aware of it and detached from it, and thus be able to see it for what it is. Through time, during meditation our thinking begins to slow down leaving appreciable gaps between thoughts. Thinking doesn't merely go away or stop entirely, and that isn't the aim of meditation, but we begin to develop a distance from it, a perspective on it. Thoughts are just thoughts, they aren't real. They aren't you. They come and go. Have patience with them.

Alternatives
If the breath is a problem, due to a head cold or asthma for instance, become aware of sounds around you, or your pulse, or use the body scan or walking meditation (below) as a basic practice. You can also use a mantra as talked about above.

Duration of Meditation
Perhaps 10–15 minutes at the start would be enough, gradually lengthening up to 20–30 minutes. Twice a day is recommended, first thing in the morning, before anything else, and in the evening, though not so late that you just fall asleep. Set a timer, put the phone on the answering machine or switch it off, go somewhere suitable. If you can't do this, do 5 minutes, or 2 minutes. But do it.

2. Walking Meditation
We must learn to take our awareness, our practice of the presence of God outside formal meditation into our lives. We can follow the breath in any gap in our routine. Setting our computer to sound a chime on the quarter hours and taking three mindful breaths in the name of the Father, Son and Holy Spirit, for example. Or doing the same thing when we stop at a traffic light. This is a good way of putting God back into our lives. We naturally push God out, and try to keep all the space to ourselves. But we can be mindful of many small actions during the day: washing our face, dressing, or waking up. Going up or down stairs. Learning to eat mindfully is a very useful thing. (See the Booklist.) But another important practice related to breathing meditation is walking meditation. It can be informal, done when we're just walking around, as a way of bringing mindfulness of the presence into our life, or else done instead of, or as well as, our formal meditation.

Our awareness may seem to be just of the ordinary things around us – sounds, sensations, tastes, feelings, emotions – but they are what make up our reality; they are where God is. God is here and now and with us in this ordinary life. Nowhere else. We expect to see him in the spectacular, or in what are classed as 'religious experiences', but we will find him quicker and closer in breathing, eating, and walking on the earth.

Formal

Find somewhere you can walk ten or more paces in a straight line. Somewhere quiet where people won't see you.

Eyes lowered, looking at the ground perhaps a metre or two ahead of you, but posture and head erect, hands clasped in front of your chest.

Take a few quieting breaths, then, inhaling, slowly lift your foot and place it a short step away. Just half the length of your foot, not much more. Feel the sensation of lifting, moving, placing; you might exhale gently as you move your weight onto the foot. Then do the next foot, feeling the whole process, breathing in time, keeping balance, feeling weight transferring onto the foot. When attention wanders, bring it back, just like ordinary meditation. At the end of your track, turn mindfully and slowly and repeat the exercise.

That's all there is to it. Awareness of your own movement.

Some people prefer this to sitting meditation. It's very good if you're agitated about something and find sitting still a problem. It's not a matter of getting anywhere, it's a matter of just being, and giving the mind something to do. Like giving it chewing gum to keep it out of mischief. It roots us strongly in the here and the now, in reality, rather than in our thoughts and ideas about it.

Variants of the technique are:

1. Slowing the whole action down. Lifting takes one inhalation, moving one exhalation, placing one inhalation, weight transfer one exhalation; all with deep concentration on the sensations felt, and perhaps mentally saying 'lifting/moving, etc.' with each breath if it helps.

2. One foot moved and placed on an inhalation, the other foot on the out-breath.

Informal

If you're out for a constitutional walk, count steps on each in-breath and out-breath at ordinary walking speeds, or silently say 'in, in, in, out, out, out' with each step, or say the Jesus Prayer with each breath or a mantra word on each step, but keeping the attention on the footfalls.

This can be done anywhere, at any time, just moving around in ordinary work or shopping in a supermarket or moving around the house.

Or become aware of your legs or your entire body moving along and keep your attention on the movement and the sensations associated with it. Keep bringing the mind gently back to the job.

This is something you could do if you're actually climbing a mountain. Climb mindfully, aware of each step as far as you are able, and aware of your breathing. But take care to stay in the moment you are existing in, where God is, rather than in your fantasies, or ideas about it all. Be on this mountain, in this place, in this moment, with God. Gently ignore all the internal discussion and commentary by constantly bringing the mind back to your feet, your breathing.

3. Body Scan

This enables us to become aware of our physicality, our actual form of existence. Emotion and thinking don't just occur in the brain, they also have a physical side. We tense bits and pieces of ourselves on and off together with our thinking and mood. All sorts of physical sensations arise when emotions pass through us. We have habitual ways of holding ourselves, of sitting, of moving, standing up and sitting down. We are a body, not just a mind, and the two are deeply tied together. So we need to pay attention to our bodies in a way we may not usually do. That way we can learn more about ourselves at a visceral level, and watch ourselves as we go through things. This isn't about relaxation, though that may be a by-product, it's about awareness and understanding at an intuitive level. There is wisdom available here, wisdom which can tell us how to work with ourselves, our feelings and with the life situations in which we find ourselves. The reality of our own existence.

Is it a form of prayer?
It is. We do it in the presence of God, open to that presence, and welcoming it within us. What we feel when we do the meditation is the life within us, the breath, the sign of the existence God has given us and breathed into us.

This is part of loving ourselves, part of Christ's commandment of loving God and our neighbour as ourselves. Without love and care for ourselves, we are incapable of loving anyone else in any realistic or healthy way. Without understanding ourselves in our physicality, how we actually function within ourselves at a mental and physical level, we are unlikely to fully understand the way anyone else thinks and behaves. This must be an integral part of any total spiritual regimen. We are not just a mind, not just a passenger in a handy, fleshy source of transport and entertainment. Our mind and body are linked, our emotions are as much physical as mental. We are a body, and we need to understand it in all its strengths and weaknesses, the pleasure it can give and its inevitable weaknesses, illnesses, ageing and death. How can we fully enter into the lives of the people around us in any realistic way if we shut ourselves out of part of our own lives? This grounds us very much in the experience of the moment, this moment in this body. Not in fantasy or mental story but here and now in reality.

This is not just a physical meditation. Spirit and body are not different things, or separate things. They coexist. We are both things simultaneously. This kind of meditation emphasises that. It is not just a mental exercise, it happens in real time, in this place, this reality, which is where and how we experience God. There is nowhere else to do that.

This meditation can stand on its own as a regular formal meditation, not just an occasional one. If you try it, it's worth doing regularly for a week or two at the start, so that you learn to do it, and begin to experience the true depth of it, rather than just a once off. All these meditations require us to learn new skills, and that doesn't come overnight.

Sit as for the breathing meditation. Or you can do it lying down as well, though beware of dozing off! Keeping your eyes open might help with drowsiness. Read over the whole text below first, so that you understand what's going on. It might be worth recording yourself reading the text very slowly so that you can play it when you do the meditation for the first couple of times, or there are CDs available online if you look. After a while you should be able to do it on your own. Again, as you go through the meditation, as your mind wanders off from time to time, gently keep returning it to the task in hand.

How fast you move through the meditation depends on yourself. It's worth leaving yourself a good chunk of time to get the full good of it the first few times you try it; perhaps half an hour or forty-five minutes. With repetition you will be able to do it with much greater facility, and be able to take in much more subtle feelings.

Close your eyes. Breathe through your nose. Spend a short while allowing your mind to settle down a bit, centring yourself. What you will be trying to become aware of is the subtle fizzing, buzzing sensation of your nerve endings that our minds usually block out. It requires concentration, and a bit of practice. You will come in on it in time. It's worth starting with a more sensitive part of your body first, until you get the idea: become aware of the tips of your fingers, where there are a lot of nerve endings. Just stay with the tips of your fingers, or of one finger, bringing your attention back if it wanders off, and after a moment or two, you should begin to be aware of a strange, mild, prickling or fizzing sensation. These are the messages from nerve endings which we aren't usually aware of. Our brains edit the information reaching our consciousness, cutting a lot of it out, or else we would be completely overloaded with distracting sensations from all parts of our bodies at once. This subtle sensation is what we're going to use as an object of concentration.

It may be a help to concentration to imagine breathing in and out of the part you're concentrating on: in through your hand, then out through your hand, for example. In some parts of your body you may just feel ordinary touch sensations, clothes, pressure, or perhaps you won't feel anything at all, but that's ok. Just allow yourself to feel the sensation of not feeling anything. With time though, you can become aware of the nerve activity all over your body.

This meditation can be done in any order. Beginning at the crown of the head, as here, or else with one of your big toes, and working up each leg separately, then back up or down again. It doesn't matter, as long as you cover every part of yourself on each sweep, giving attention to each area, one after the other. It's best to work out an order that suits you, and stick to that.

Meditation
Begin now by taking your attention to the top of your head. Become aware of any sensations in your scalp; perhaps

imagine the breath entering and leaving your scalp. Take your time and allow all the sensations to arise. There is no rush. Spend at least a few full breaths on each part of the body. Then move on to your forehead. Be aware of any sensations, or tensions; spend a few full inhalations and exhalations doing that. Then move on to your eyes, take a few breaths there; now the nose, take a few breaths there; now bring the attention to the mouth and lips, take a few breaths; now the chin and lower jaw, take a few breaths there. Now be aware of the ears and sides of the head, breathing gently in and out for a few breaths. Now the back of the head, the neck. Is there any tension, any pain? Don't move, just be aware, breathing. Now the front of the neck, the throat.

Move on to the right shoulder, the upper arm, the forearms and wrist, gradually moving down a section at a time. Take your time. Feel everything. Now the hand: start with the little finger, breath into and out of it, if that helps, and be aware of the sensations in it; now the ring finger, the middle finger, the index finger, the thumb; now the palm of the hand, the back of the hand; now the whole hand.

Now we take our attention to the left shoulder, the upper arm, the forearms and wrist. Now the hand: the individual fingers, the palm of the hand, the back of the hand; now the whole hand.

Now we become aware of the upper back; perhaps the feeling of the chair on our shoulder blades, our clothes, and then more subtle sensation. And now the chest area; perhaps we can feel the movement of the chest with the breath going in and out. Now the lower back; now the belly, moving with the breath; now the lower abdomen; now the buttocks. Feel the pressure of the chair, your weight bearing down, then look for the more subtle sensations.

Now the left thigh, the knee, the calf of the leg, the shin, the ankle, the heel, the bottom of the foot, the big toe, the smaller toes (can you distinguish each one?), the top of the foot.

Now the right thigh, the knee, the calf of the leg, the shin the ankle, the heel, the bottom of the foot, the big toe, the smaller toes, the top of the foot.

Now become aware, as best you can, of the whole body, living, breathing from top to toe, the envelope of your skin, the sensations on your skin; small fleeting pains, tingling, pressure; all of it. Then begin with the big toe on your left foot, and work your way back up the body, a bit at a time, gently bringing attention back to the task at hand as the mind wanders.

After practice you may be able to do the whole process more smoothly, and effectively; speed is not necessarily to be aimed for. Spend extra time with any part of the body that has a pain or ache. Just become aware of the pain, breathe in and out through it, and become aware of the nature of it, the complexity of it, what the pain actually is, what it 'looks' like in your mind. Spend time with it, then move on. At the end of the meditation, gently come back to the room again, opening your eyes. Try to take the awareness of feeling with you as you go through the day.

4. Metta, or Lovingkindness Meditation

This meditation also comes from the Buddhist tradition, and it is a very important technique for Christians to learn. Christ taught that we should be loving, his teaching and life was set in terms of love. That's what this meditation teaches you – how to love people, all and any people, including yourself. It is as simple as that. Jesus, unfortunately, didn't leave us any instructions or hints on *how* to go about loving our enemies, or people who hurt us or do bad things to us, or how to love neighbours we don't like. It's obvious this isn't an easy thing to do. The word 'love' and the word 'enemy' don't sit beside each other very well. This meditation can begin to train our minds and hearts to work better. Like practising a golf swing or playing music, we can practise loving people.

Many of us need to learn to love. But very rarely did anyone ever tell you that, or help you to learn, or show you a way. We are simply commanded and expected to love and be loving, but it doesn't always come naturally to all of us. Some of us grew up in houses where love wasn't openly displayed, or possibly even present. But we can still learn, whatever age we are. This meditation can make your heart bigger, until it could perhaps hold the whole world in it just like God does. This in itself brings with it insight and enrichment in terms of forgiveness, acceptance and generosity.

This can be, and is traditionally used briefly to finish a formal meditation session, or as an entire, regular formal meditation in itself. It can be used informally when you're out walking around, on the bus or train, in a hospital, or when you're bored at a meeting. Direct it at random people you come across. Wish them well. Why not? Normally we are either attracted to and interested in another person, or feel antagonistic towards them in some way, or else we are completely neutral towards them. All this based on a very brief glance and a lot of subconscious judgement. We're influenced by sexual attraction, class, clothes, accent, the way people walk. But we are not to judge people, Christ said, we are to love them. This is how to learn to do that.

Lovingkindness meditation can be a help or an antidote when you are feeling very angry, or afraid, or a strong dislike of someone, or are finding it hard to forgive someone – or yourself. Simply say the words in time with your breathing, and direct your love and care towards the person. This can begin to change our mind and heart, to dissolve old judgements and opinions, and allow reality in. We can also use it when perhaps someone is very ill or in trouble far away from us, when we may feel helpless and worried.

Will this meditation have any effect on the other person, will it do *them* any good? We've discussed this before in terms of prayer or forgiveness. What we can be sure of is that it is good for you, it will change you, and that's as much of the world as you have power to change. Let that be enough for you, because you'll have your work cut out doing that much alone! Leave the rest to God.

Lovingkindness as a formal meditation or as part of one can be done in the same posture as for breathing meditation, or lying down, or walking. When doing it on your own, say the lines in time with the breath. The words below are not specifically prescribed, feel free to alter or simplify them to suit yourself or the situation.

We start with ourselves, which seems strange in our culture. We're inclined to take Christ's order to 'deny ourselves' in a very literal (wrong) way, which means we feel we have to cut ourselves out of the picture entirely in some kind of weird humility. That's not actually what Christ meant, and it's not a good thing for us to do. Denying yourself has a deeper spiritual meaning. But at the level of ordinary life, we need to love ourselves. Christ's commandment was to love God, and to love your neighbour as *yourself*. Love of ourselves is allowed and expected and is part of healthy psychology. We matter. God loves us, and we have to love us too. Many of us have no idea even how to start.

The kind of love we're talking about here isn't a mushy, sentimental thing. It is not about nice feelings. This sort of love is about care and consideration, acceptance and compassion.

We need to show that to ourselves as well as to other people. Children learn and grow and mature best when they are loved and cared for and accepted for what they are. Even as adults we too will do best in the light of our own compassion and love for ourselves, our acceptance of ourselves for what we are. Then we can grow and mature and change all the more.

If it would help, replace the word 'love' with 'friendliness'. Love as a word, a concept, is pretty threadbare in our culture, and might not resonate with many people in the right way. Christ spoke in terms of love but he also talked in terms of friendship.

> This is my commandment, that you love one another as I have loved you. No one has greater love than this, to lay down one's life for one's friends. You are my friends if you do what I command you. I do not call you servants any longer, because the servant does not know what the master is doing; but I have called you friends, because I have made known to you everything that I have heard from my Father.
>
> *(John 15)*

Friendship is about acceptance and understanding. It doesn't make judgements, it implies equality, heartfelt warmth and caring attention. It is to do with opening our heart, and that's what we're about here.

We are trying to love, and take in the totality of ourselves and the other person, the truth of them. All of us consist of layers and depths, masks and cores. All of us are swayed by urges and fears, desires and dislikes. Every single one of us. These same basic mechanisms drive us all, and power our egos, and we need to understand that, and see it in ourselves and in everyone around us. We judge people on the brief glimpses and experiences we have of them, and they of us. But there is always much more going on than that. We ourselves would like and hope to be understood by others in our own confused complexity. Perhaps only God can fully do that for anyone, but we are called to try. We are called, commanded by Christ, to make our hearts grow to take cognisance of more than outward appearance, more than a positive or negative encounter with a person. This realisation and understanding of the complexity of each of us is at the root of love, the root of forgiveness and acceptance.

Meditation

Picture yourself in your own mind, perhaps as you are now, or if that seems difficult, remember yourself as you were as a young child. Innocent, free. Feel caring towards yourself, surround yourself with benevolent attention. God commands us to love ourselves. Mentally recite the words in time with your breathing:

> May I be peaceful in body and spirit.
> May I be free from injury, may I live in safety.
> May I be free from fear, anxiety and worry.
> May I be well, may I be happy.

Please spend a few minutes doing this. It may feel strange at the beginning. It isn't about nice feelings; it's about paying considerate, caring, and compassionate attention. Try to focus on the meaning of the words as you recite them. The intention alone is important. If your attention wanders, as with the other meditations, simply gently bring it back to the work in hand.

You can spend a while doing this for yourself. It takes and needs practice to begin to understand it. Indeed you can take this on as a regular formal meditation practice each day for a couple of weeks, and the same with the other sections of the meditation. Just doing it once for a couple of moments is not enough. This is a way to *practise*, and that means repetition. It is not an instant cure for anything. Change takes time.

Now think of someone you love or like; it may be one of your family, relatives or friends. Perhaps someone who needs a bit of love at the minute. Once again, perhaps it is easier to think of them when they were a young child, and had all their life before them. Let caring consideration come up in you, in your heart, and direct it to this person:

> May you be peaceful in body and spirit.
> May you be free from injury, may you live in safety.
> May you be free from fear, anxiety and worry.
> May you be well, may you be happy.

Once more, spend a while doing this.

Now think of a person for whom you feel neutral. The person who drives the bus, a person who lives near you, a person you know to see in a shop. Think of them, of the problems and happy times they have in their lives. If it helps, remember them as they were when a child. And direct lovingkindness towards them:

> May you be peaceful in body and spirit.
> May you be free from injury, may you live in safety.
> May you be free from fear, anxiety and worry.
> May you be well, may you be happy.

Think of someone traditionally termed an 'enemy'. Someone you don't like, and when you think of them, pain, anger, hurt or disgust arises in you. Even someone you just have trouble dealing with. Think of the hard things they may go through in their lives, and that they too will have happy times. The complex fears and needs they have, just like you. If it helps, think of them as a young child, innocent, with no harm in them, and remember that this is the same person. Wish them the same love you wished the others. Our Lord commanded us to love God, to love our neighbours, and our enemies.

May you be peaceful in body and spirit.
May you be free from injury, may you live in safety.
May you be free from fear, anxiety and worry.
May you be well, may you be happy.

In the Buddhist tradition, the practice would be to go on beyond this to include all sentient beings in existence. There is no harm in doing that! This can stretch the boundaries of our hearts to let more fit inside. You can do this meditation for anyone, alive or dead. It may bring peace to a bereaved heart, and promote healing.

If you are using this as a formal meditation in itself, you could try to time each part so that the period is divided equally between them. Or else do a certain number of repetitions of each, and then go back to the beginning and cycle through again for your time period. Stay longer with any particular facet if you feel there is more work to do on it. Or perhaps focus on one type only in each session over a week or two as mentioned above. Again, adjusting the words to suit, you can direct lovingkindness at different groups and kinds of people, as well as individuals. You can make it part of your walking meditation, reciting the words towards yourself or others in time with your steps or breathing. Do use it out in the world about your ordinary business, in the workplace, on the bus or in the shops; as you meet someone, informally direct lovingkindness towards them, whoever they are, and however their life is.

As well as the usual distractions experienced in any meditation, difficulties especially may arise doing this meditation for enemies. Be gentle with yourself, and perhaps try to concentrate on the good that every human has in them, however obscured or hidden it may be. If feelings and emotions arise, recognise and acknowledge them, then try to gently let go of them and return to the words.

Difficulties during Meditation or Prayer

We can understand the hardships of travel. It might be, for instance, going up a mountain when we aren't too fit. Painful legs, pumping heart, gasping, sore lungs and throat, blisters, blinded by sweat, soaked by rain, roasted by sun, and then we have to come back down again; all this perhaps with other people who are talking rubbish, getting in the way, making stupid suggestions and getting on one's nerves, which is bad enough.

On the other hand, sitting meditating or praying quietly in the comfort of one's own home has its own difficulties, its own pains and distractions to surmount. Spinning thoughts, sore limbs, doubts, frustrations, phantom itches and aches. These can seem higher obstacles than any mountain. Once we're up the mountain we have to go through with it, but in our own homes, the temptation to stop, to stand up and walk away is strong, and our minds are so quick, we may have got up and left before we even realise it ourselves. For many people, meditation will seem to consist of little more than bringing the mind back to the business in hand. Millions and millions of times. But that's what we're supposed to be doing. It works!

Practice and experience obviously help, and it might be worth seeking out a meditation group in your area, and discussing things with people there. Failing that, what follows might help a bit.

Distractions come in many forms, like itches or urges to move, or thoughts, or finding yourself having spent most of the time mentally very far away. Or drowsiness. For the last one, a good night's sleep can help, or else meditating standing up, or some deep breaths, or washing your face. Realise too that drowsiness is one way your mind tries to avoid things it doesn't like. One thing you can do is just watch and examine the sensation of drowsiness, how it starts, what the symptoms are. Get interested, and it may go away. So too with anxiety or restlessness or boredom. Just watch. How does it feel, where are the sensations arising, what are they? This too is meditation. Then after a while, return to the object of your meditation.

Thoughts can be shooed along by just labelling them. Notice, be aware that you're thinking, and just mentally say 'thinking about ...' (it may be 'memories' or 'fighting with so and so' or 'making the dinner'). Put a name on it, then you can begin to understand *how* you think, but even the mere action of recognising a thought as a thought is enough to make it stop. Understand that you will do this millions of times as a meditator, and some days will be worse than others. It's wrong to think in terms of improving, though you may acquire some skills along the way. Better perhaps to talk in terms of learning acceptance, learning to see clearly, to understand. It's more a matter of loving care for oneself, of realising our own nature as it is. Gentle, clear perception and understanding can affect us more than many good intentions ever will.

Distracting physical sensations, itches and low-level pains, for instance, should be watched for a while. Just sit with them, and breathe through them for a few breaths, and notice the kind of them, notice the urge to scratch or move or adjust position that arises in connection with them, what mental images of them occur to you, then return to your object, whatever it is. Watching teaches us much. Don't judge or comment or think about it. Just watch. Everything comes, and then goes away. Just watch.

Don't try too hard. There is nowhere to go except here, so there is no prize for getting there faster. You are there already, you are in and of God, so what we are doing is just realising that. Making it real for ourselves. In a sense, you have arrived even before you start. God loves you. What's the problem? Our mind, our ego doesn't like that. It wants to be the only show in town, go places, do things, be the best! So it creates obstacles for us, including trying too hard! Be gentle with yourself, but firm. Don't judge or beat yourself up. Just watch, and then return to the object of your meditation. Recognise, acknowledge and accept all that arises within you without judgement. Realise that this is what and how you are in your totality. Have mercy, love and compassion for yourself. As God does. Success and failure are besides the point: the intention, the returning again and again to our object is the thing. Perhaps even if all we can manage some days is the intention to have an intention! There are books in the Booklist with good information on obstacles to meditation which may be of help to you.

Let Out Clause
All that said, meditation may not actually suit everybody. It is not easy, it is not the catch-all cure for everything that ails you that some people would have you believe, and there may be times in your life where it may not be the best thing for you to do. It *is* worth trying and finding out about, but different people have different needs depending on their background and nature. Vocal prayer on the other hand suits everybody, even if it is not always easy either! The sense of proportion and connection it can bring, the deepening relationship with the God who loves us and is already a part of us, in whom we live

and move and exist, is an important part of being human, of being who we are in our deepest totality.

Teachers

If you can, it's a good idea to get help and instruction from someone who has been down the path of meditation and prayer before you. You can at the very least lose heart and get bewildered and discouraged. You can also get stuck in one place, or wander off in irrelevant directions. A good teacher can be a good example, an adviser and director. There are people out there trained in spiritual guidance.

There are also meditation groups you could join. It's hard to keep up a solo practice without some companionship. Books can help, and there are recommendations at the back of this one, but other humans are necessary too. Most people find that meditation and prayer, even in silence, if done in company with other people is remarkably easier and more effective.

CHAPTER EIGHT

Stations

The word 'station' means a place to stop. The entire mountain is a stopping place, a station, in one sense, because we come here to stop whatever else it is we are doing: the mad rush of our lives, the incessant stimulation of TV and music and computer and email and mobile, calls and texts, messages and reminders. On the mountain, the phone is off (or should be!), the computer is miles away. 'They' can't get us, and our mind is our own for a short while, and we stop.

Or we try to. It might take a while for the mad whirl of your brain to subside, for mental texts, reminders and emails to stop arriving, for us to stop worrying or organising or planning. To stop reviewing what has happened, or what is supposed to happen. We even bring those organisational, planning skills, or perhaps drives would be the better word, up the mountain; the day is supposed to be like this, this is supposed to happen, and then this, and we are going to feel like this and this. Anything else happening will be a disappointment, a let down, a Bad Thing.

What we need to do is just be here and take it as it comes, good and bad, wet and dry, clouds or clear sky. It is usually summed up nowadays in the clichéd, catch-all term 'Relax'. We know what that means, or we think we do, but we may find it an elusive thing to achieve. At its most straightforward, it may simply mean accepting whatever and however things are. To switch off planning, and fixing and improving and making better. Just accept. Just be here, now. Easier said than done. But station means stop. Whether it's blisters or beauty, exhilaration or tiredness, dry or damp, let it be that way. Stop trying to fix it or bewail it, just live it.

As we ascend the mountain we can stop at stations along the route. We can use the traditional *leachtanna*, the 'penitential beds', or we can stop where and when and as often as we like. Perhaps when breath or stamina oblige us. When we stop for a station, there are things we can do; either the traditional rounds with their accompanying prayers, or silent meditation, or Bible readings, or other meditations, like the Stations of the Cross, or the Stations of Joy, or of Healing, for example. The action of performing rounds at the traditional stations is still worth doing, whatever prayers, or meditations we are saying or following at the time. The repetition, the movement, the focus, all help, all work, all do something for us.

In the absence of traditional cairns and penitential beds, on your own mountain, perhaps it would be worth choosing some object, a stone, a tree, an icon carried with you, as the centre of a circumambulation (although passers by in a public place will be, at the very least, intrigued). In your own quiet place at home, coming and sitting down and saying your prayers or meditating or doing walking meditation is also a station, a time to stop. Or you can simply stop for a few breaths in the middle of work or whatever you're doing, and bring your mind back to where you are, and to your physical sensations or your breathing – and the presence of God. You could say a short prayer if that feels right. Use stations in the middle of the pilgrimage of ordinary life. Try to see Sunday worship as a station, a resting place of prayer, in the flow of the journey of your existence.

What we do with our minds between the stations is important. We can let them roam free, but we could do that on any walk or dander. On pilgrimage, on the mountain, we must be more constructive. Either we focus on something physical – our breathing, our walking and movement – or on a prayer word, or short prayer – the Jesus Prayer, a mantra, the Rosary, a word or phrase or idea from a reading or meditation we've just heard or read at the last station. Or we could perhaps follow one of the discursive meditations, the Stations of Reality. Always bringing our minds back to now, to this place and this time and this experience. Not analysing it, but living it. Not working out what it means, but going through it, being it.

It is possible to just be where we are, walking, breathing, one step after another, keeping our minds on the reality of this moment, and then this moment, then this one, one after another. It takes practice and experience to stop the mind from wandering away from something or somewhere it doesn't like, or that doesn't stimulate us enough. A simple object of concentration, the breath, a prayer, a footstep, an idea we are exploring, will fasten the mind for a while and provide a thread of continuity in our experience. Even then we will have to return again and again to our object.

For most of us, for most of the time, that in itself will be meditation; returning, and returning over and over to whatever-it-is. What that teaches us is to return to real life, to reality, to the place where God is. What this skill is useful for in a spiritual sense is finding God. Because God is here and now, always. We are rarely here and now, we are mostly elsewhere, and otherwise, and wishing things were different, or dwelling on how they used to be. Returning again and again to the object of concentration brings us back to reality, back to the place were God is. (Have a look at *Practice of the Presence of God*. See the Booklist.) The intention, the constant returning is perhaps more important than success.

The stations most familiar for many people are the traditional Stations of the Cross. This is a way of meditating on passages of scripture, or events from Christ's life, while moving around, individually, or as a group, or in formal procession. We can do that here if we wish, but the format can be modified indefinitely, as in the Stations of Healing, below. It can be used while moving around, on the mountain or in a church. It can also be used where you are, staying in one place, but using the meditations and readings to divide up time, rather than space or distance.

It is envisaged that people would keep silence in between each station, keeping in mind the images arising from it, or perhaps a phrase, or a word, or a feeling, returning to it repeatedly when distractions arise, or thoughts stray.

This is a good form of moving meditation, which can give structure to pilgrimage, whether that be long or short. It can keep bringing our minds back to the point of what we are doing, what we are there for, and turn a walk into a spiritual exercise.

Stations are Meditations
Meditation on the Cross and on Christ's Passion grew to become a popular devotion in the high to late middle ages, and predates and informs the Stations of the Cross commonly found today in many churches. The cultural move within Western Christianity during that time was one of developing compassion for the suffering Christ rather than fear of God. Suffering *with* Christ, in effect. The modern devotion of the

Stations of the Cross grows naturally out of this. There is still benefit in these days for growing compassion in oneself. What is also needed in our time is a new way of talking about what Christ did and does on the Cross, what it means, and what the deeper layers of it are. The older explanations of the Cross carry less and less weight and credibility for people of our Western culture, but the meanings underlying it still need to be brought into the light and words of our times, for the ears and hearts of our contemporaries. Through contemplation of the suffering Christ, this is possible for each of us, watching, seeing, being with Christ as he hangs on the Cross. The first set of stations are of great worth for this.

The Stations of Joy, or of the Resurrection, are a more recent important balance to the previous set. If we reduce Christ to a figure on a cross undertaking one specific action, however important, we have done our faith a disservice. Christ had a life and a teaching before his Passion and death, and there is life and teaching in his resurrection as well. The Resurrection can be a stumbling block for some Christians of our time, and is perhaps only capable of being understood by us through contemplation and meditation.

One thing we can seek to learn is to allow the question to abide. Rather than looking for simple, or even complicated, answers, in order to bring a process of questioning to an end, as we usually do, deep ideas such as the Passion, Death and Resurrection of Christ require different treatment. The word the Church used for such things was mysteries. The word no longer means the same as it once did, but the concept is important. There are some things which are not capable of being expressed in words. Not that we cannot comprehend them at some level, but any deep understanding of them will be personal and nearly impossible to express to another person in a way they could understand unless they had gone to the same place themselves. Allowing the question to abide brings us before Christ on the Cross, or Christ Risen, or Jesus the Healer and Teacher, with an unvoiced question, which allows exploration, penetrative understanding, and opening to a great depth. The simple answers are never simple, the complicated answers may simply obscure the truth, and the truth may not fit into words. There is no final, simple, or even complicated answer; finding out, understanding, is the work of an entire lifetime, the point of prayer and meditation.

Devotional sets of stations such as these can be a different kind of meditation, allowing us to sit with Jesus, face to face, and begin to understand or at least begin to explore what he means. Here, in Christ's eyes, we can see the incarnation of love, compassion, self-giving and self-sacrifice, obedience, and vulnerability. We can begin to understand who we are in ourselves and in relation to Christ. We may receive the grace to enunciate the significance of Christ and the Cross in words and ideas that people of our time can grasp and intuit.

The Traditional Stations

The traditional stations performed at various holy sites in Ireland were designed originally for people who could not read, and so they amount to a simple series of various short prayers repeated. The Hail Mary, the Creed, the Gloria, the Our Father, all in various combinations. The prayers would be said at each bed or cairn or station in the pilgrimage. I give here the traditional form of the stations for Cruach Phádraig, for those who might get the chance to use them, or would be interested to try. The general format on Lough Derg in Donegal, for example, or in Reilig Ghobnatan in Cúil Aodha in West Cork, and in all the other holy sites of this country is much the same; visiting the various beds or *leachtanna* in a certain order and saying the prayers in specific numbers or combinations. The beds (depending where you are, these may be hut circles, large stones or cairns of stones) are circled while saying the prayers, always clockwise, *deiseal*, with the person's right side towards whatever it is they are circling. Traditionally a number of small stones were gathered at each bed at the beginning, as an aid to counting the correct number of circumambulations when the mind is elsewhere. One stone is tossed down for each turn. Such rounds were often accompanied by additional mortifications; on Lough Derg, for example, they are done on the knees, as used to be the case on Cruach Phádraig; the mountain is still sometimes climbed barefoot by a number of people. Given the nature of the terrain on the mountain, especially at the top, the chances of minor injury are not inconsiderable. For modern people who have lived their lives in shoes this is a very painful procedure, possibly dangerous, and much forethought and care must go into any decision to walk this way.

Many people traditionally recite the Rosary between stations, but you could use the Jesus Prayer, or a mantra if you find that is an aid to your attention. (See Chapter Eight.) It should be emphasised again that the actual numbers of prayers, the repetition, is unimportant in the end; it is the connection achieved, the depth of attention, that is the thing; the time spent in God's company, the strengthening and deepening of relationship through prayer.

Traditional Stations on Croagh Patrick

The first traditional station is at the base of the cone, Leacht Benáin. The pilgrim walks seven times clockwise around the cairn saying seven Our Fathers, seven Hail Marys and one Creed.

The summit is the second station. The pilgrim there kneels and says seven Our Fathers, seven Hail Marys and one Creed; then walks, clockwise, fifteen times around the Chapel saying fifteen Our Fathers, fifteen Hail Marys, and one Creed; then walks seven times around Leaba Phádraig saying seven Our Fathers, seven Hail Marys and one Creed.

The third station is Reilig Mhuire on the western side of the mountain. Here the pilgrim says seven Our Fathers, seven Hail Marys and one Creed while walking around each cairn seven times; then seven times around the whole enclosure seven times, praying.

The Way of the Cross

The Stations of the Cross have a long tradition within the Church, going back to the time when pilgrims to Jerusalem in very ancient times used to follow the path from Pilate's house to Calvary. The tradition came home with them to their own countries.

The number of stations has varied over the years. The version given here is an ecumenical one, based solely on scripture, which is accessible to all Christian traditions, but of course please feel free to stick to what you are most used to.

These stations may be used on the way up the mountain, when we take a breather, or on the journey to or from our sacred place, or during a walk. We can use them sitting in one place, on our own or with a group. These stations are written as a liturgy for a group of people; on your own, just say all the words. At the space for reflection you may pray silently, or meditate, or do Lectio Divina on what you've just heard. The following stations are from the Church of England, *Times and Seasons* (p. 236).

The Gathering

The ministers enter in silence.

In the name of the Father,
and of the Son,
and of the Holy Spirit.
All Amen.

Jesus told his disciples, 'If any want to become my followers, let them deny themselves and take up their cross and follow me. For those who want to save their life will lose it, and those who lose their life for my sake will find it.' (*Matthew 16:24–25*)

Once we were far off, but now in union with Christ Jesus we have been brought near through the shedding of Christ's blood, for he is our peace. (*Ephesians 2:13–14*)

An appropriate greeting may be given.

A minister may introduce the service and then says

Let us pray.

A brief moment of silence follows.

Almighty and everlasting God,
who in your tender love towards the human race
sent your Son our Saviour Jesus Christ
to take upon him our flesh
and to suffer death upon the cross:
grant that we may follow the example of his patience
and humility,
and also be made partakers of his resurrection;
through Jesus Christ your Son our Lord,
who is alive and reigns with you,
in the unity of the Holy Spirit,
one God, now and for ever.

All Amen.

All Holy God,
holy and strong,
holy and immortal,
have mercy upon us.

First Station: Jesus in agony in the Garden of Gethsemane

We adore you, O Christ, and we bless you,
All because by your holy cross you have redeemed the
world.

Reading
A reading from the Gospel according to Mark.

They went to a place called Gethsemane; and he said to
his disciples, 'Sit here while I pray.' He took with him
Peter and James and John, and began to be distressed
and agitated. And he said to them, 'I am deeply grieved,
even to death; remain here, and keep awake.' And going
a little farther, he threw himself on the ground and
prayed that, if it were possible, the hour might pass
from him. He said, 'Abba, Father, for you all things are
possible; remove this cup from me; yet, not what I want,
but what you want.' (*Mark 14:32–6*)

A Reflection, or period of silence may follow.

Prayer
Lord Jesus, you entered the garden of fear
and faced the agony of your impending death:
be with those who share that agony
and face death unwillingly this day.
You shared our fear
and knew the weakness of our humanity:
give strength and hope to the dispirited and despairing.
To you, Jesus, who sweated blood,
be honour and glory with the Father and the Holy Spirit,
now and for ever.
All Amen.

All Holy God,
    holy and strong,
    holy and immortal,
    have mercy upon us.

Second Station: Jesus betrayed by Judas and arrested

    We adore you, O Christ, and we bless you,
All because by your holy cross you have redeemed the
    world.

    Reading
    A reading from the Gospel according to Mark.

    Immediately, while he was still speaking, Judas, one of
    the twelve, arrived; and with him there was a crowd
    with swords and clubs, from the chief priests, the scribes,
    and the elders. Now the betrayer had given them a sign,
    saying, 'The one I will kiss is the man; arrest him and
    lead him away under guard.' So when he came, he went
    up to him at once and said, 'Rabbi!' and kissed him.
    Then they laid hands on him and arrested him. (*Mark
    14:43–6*)

    A Reflection, or period of silence may follow.

    Prayer
    Lord Jesus, you were betrayed by the kiss of a friend:
    be with those who are betrayed and slandered
    and falsely accused.
    You knew the experience of having your love
    thrown back in your face for mere silver:
    be with families which are torn apart
    by mistrust or temptation.

To you, Jesus, who offered your face to your betrayer,
be honour and glory with the Father and the Holy Spirit,
now and for ever.
All Amen.

All Holy God,
holy and strong,
holy and immortal,
have mercy upon us.

Third Station: Jesus condemned by the Sanhedrin

We adore you, O Christ, and we bless you,
All because by your holy cross you have redeemed the
world.

Reading
A reading from the Gospel according to Mark.

Now the chief priests and the whole council were
looking for testimony against Jesus to put him to death;
but they found none. For many gave false testimony
against him, and their testimony did not agree. Some
stood up and gave false testimony against him, saying,
'We heard him say, "I will destroy this temple that is
made with hands, and in three days I will build another,
not made with hands".' But even on this point their
testimony did not agree. Then the high priest stood up
before them and asked Jesus, 'Have you no answer?
What is it that they testify against you?' But he was
silent and did not answer. Again the high priest asked
him, 'Are you the Messiah, the Son of the Blessed One?'
Jesus said, 'I am; and "you will see the Son of Man
seated at the right hand of the Power", and "coming

with the clouds of heaven".' Then the high priest tore his clothes and said, 'Why do we still need witnesses? You have heard his blasphemy! What is your decision?' All of them condemned him as deserving death. (*Mark 14:55–64*)

A Reflection, or period of silence may follow.

Prayer
Lord Jesus, you were the victim of religious bigotry:
be with those who are persecuted
by small-minded authority.
You faced the condemnation of fearful hearts:
deepen the understanding of those
who shut themselves off
from the experience and wisdom of others.
To you, Jesus, unjustly judged victim,
be honour and glory with the Father and the Holy Spirit,
now and for ever.
All Amen.

All Holy God,
holy and strong,
holy and immortal,
have mercy upon us.

Fourth Station: Peter denies Jesus

We adore you, O Christ, and we bless you,
All because by your holy cross you have redeemed the world.

Reading
A reading from the Gospel according to Mark.

At that moment the cock crowed for the second time. Then Peter remembered that Jesus had said to him,

'Before the cock crows twice, you will deny me three times.' And he broke down and wept. (*Mark 14:72*)

A Reflection, or period of silence may follow.

Prayer
Lord Jesus, as Peter betrayed you,
you experienced the double agony of love rejected
and friendship denied:
be with those who know no friends
and are rejected by society.
You understood the fear within Peter:
help us to understand the anxieties
of those who fear for their future.
To you, Jesus,
who gazed with sadness at your lost friend,
be honour and glory with the Father and the Holy Spirit,
now and for ever.
All Amen.

All Holy God,
holy and strong,
holy and immortal,
have mercy upon us.

Fifth Station: Jesus judged by Pilate

We adore you, O Christ, and we bless you,
All because by your holy cross you have redeemed the world.

Reading
A reading from the Gospel according to Mark.

Pilate asked them, 'Why, what evil has he done?' But they shouted all the more, 'Crucify him!' So Pilate,

wishing to satisfy the crowd, released Barabbas for
them; and after flogging Jesus, he handed him over to be
crucified. (*Mark 15:14–15*)

A Reflection, or period of silence may follow.

Prayer
Lord Jesus,
you were condemned to death for political expediency:
be with those
who are imprisoned for the convenience of the powerful.
You were the victim of unbridled injustice:
change the minds and motivations
of oppressors and exploiters to your way of peace.
To you, Jesus, innocent though condemned,
be honour and glory with the Father and the Holy Spirit,
now and for ever.
All   Amen.

All   Holy God,
holy and strong,
holy and immortal,
have mercy upon us.

Sixth Station: Jesus scourged and crowned with thorns

We adore you, O Christ, and we bless you,
All   because by your holy cross you have redeemed the
world.

Reading
A reading from the Gospel according to Mark.
And they clothed him in a purple cloak; and after
twisting some thorns into a crown, they put it on him.
And they began saluting him, 'Hail, King of the Jews!'

They struck his head with a reed, spat upon him, and knelt down in homage to him. (*Mark 15:17–19*)

A Reflection, or period of silence may follow.

Prayer
Lord Jesus, you faced the torment of barbaric punishment and mocking tongue:
be with those who cry out in physical agony and emotional distress.
You endured unbearable abuse:
be with those who face torture and mockery in our world today.
To you, Jesus, the King crowned with thorns,
be honour and glory with the Father and the Holy Spirit,
now and for ever.
All Amen.

All Holy God,
holy and strong,
holy and immortal,
have mercy upon us.

Seventh Station: Jesus carries the cross

We adore you, O Christ, and we bless you,
All because by your holy cross you have redeemed the world.

Reading
A reading from the Gospel according to Mark.

After mocking him, they stripped him of the purple cloak and put his own clothes on him. Then they led him out to crucify him. (*Mark 15:20*)

161

A Reflection, or period of silence may follow.

Prayer
Lord Jesus,
you carried the cross through the rough streets of Jerusalem:
be with those
who are loaded with burdens beyond their strength.
You bore the weight of our sins
when you carried the cross:
help us to realize the extent
and the cost of your love for us.
To you, Jesus, bearing a cross not your own,
be honour and glory with the Father and the Holy Spirit,
now and for ever.
All Amen.

All Holy God,
holy and strong,
holy and immortal,
have mercy upon us.

Eighth Station: Simon of Cyrene helps Jesus to carry the cross

We adore you, O Christ, and we bless you,
All because by your holy cross you have redeemed the
world.

Reading
A reading from the Gospel according to Mark.

They compelled a passer-by, who was coming in from
the country, to carry his cross; it was Simon of Cyrene,
the father of Alexander and Rufus. (*Mark 15:21*)

A Reflection, or period of silence may follow.

Prayer
Lord Jesus, you were worn down by fatigue:
be with those from whom life drains all energy.
You needed the help of a passing stranger:
give us the humility to receive aid from others.
To you, Jesus, weighed down with exhaustion
and in need of help,
be honour and glory with the Father and the Holy Spirit,
now and for ever.
All Amen.

All Holy God,
holy and strong,
holy and immortal,
have mercy upon us.

Ninth Station: Jesus meets the women of Jerusalem

We adore you, O Christ, and we bless you,
All because by your holy cross you have redeemed the
world.

Reading
A reading from the Gospel according to Luke.

A great number of the people followed him, and among
them were women who were beating their breasts and
wailing for him. But Jesus turned to them and said,
'Daughters of Jerusalem, do not weep for me, but weep
for yourselves and for your children. For the days are
surely coming when they will say, "Blessed are the
barren, and the wombs that never bore, and the breasts
that never nursed." Then they will begin to say to the
mountains, "Fall on us"; and to the hills, "Cover us." For

if they do this when the wood is green, what will
happen when it is dry?' (*Luke 23:27–31*)

A Reflection, or period of silence may follow.

Prayer
Lord Jesus, the women of Jerusalem wept for you:
move us to tears at the plight of the broken in our world.
You embraced the pain of Jerusalem, the 'city of peace':
bless Jerusalem this day
and lead it to the path of profound peace.
To you, Jesus, the King of peace
who wept for the city of peace,
be honour and glory with the Father and the Holy Spirit,
now and for ever.
All Amen.

All Holy God,
   holy and strong,
   holy and immortal,
   have mercy upon us.

Tenth Station: Jesus is crucified

We adore you, O Christ, and we bless you,
All because by your holy cross you have redeemed the
   world.

Reading
A reading from the Gospel according to Mark.

And they crucified him, and divided his clothes among
them, casting lots to decide what each should take.
(*Mark 15:24*)

164

A Reflection, or period of silence may follow.

Prayer
Lord Jesus, you bled in pain
as the nails were driven into your flesh:
transform through the mystery of your love
the pain of those who suffer.
To you, Jesus, our crucified Lord,
be honour and glory with the Father and the Holy Spirit,
now and for ever.
All Amen.

All Holy God,
holy and strong,
holy and immortal,
have mercy upon us.

Eleventh Station: Jesus promises the kingdom to the penitent thief

We adore you, O Christ, and we bless you,
All because by your holy cross you have redeemed the
world.

Reading
A reading from the Gospel according to Luke.

One of the criminals who were hanged there kept
deriding him and saying, 'Are you not the Messiah?
Save yourself and us!' But the other rebuked him, saying,
'Do you not fear God, since you are under the same
sentence of condemnation? And we indeed have been
condemned justly, for we are getting what we deserve
for our deeds, but this man has done nothing wrong.'

Then he said, 'Jesus, remember me when you come into your kingdom.' He replied, 'Truly I tell you, today you will be with me in Paradise.' (*Luke 23:39–43*)

A Reflection, or period of silence may follow.

Prayer
Lord Jesus,
even in your deepest agony you listened to the crucified thief:
hear us as we unburden to you our deepest fears.
You spoke words of love in your hour of death:
help us to speak words of life to a dying world.
To you, Jesus, who offer hope to the hopeless,
be honour and glory with the Father and the Holy Spirit,
now and for ever.
All Amen.

All Holy God,
holy and strong,
holy and immortal,
have mercy upon us.

Twelfth Station: Jesus on the cross; his mother and his friend

We adore you, O Christ, and we bless you,
All because by your holy cross you have redeemed the world.

Reading
A reading from the Gospel according to John.

When Jesus saw his mother and the disciple whom he loved standing beside her, he said to his mother,

'Woman, here is your son.' Then he said to the disciple, 'Here is your mother.' And from that hour the disciple took her into his own home. (*John 19:26–7*)

A Reflection, or period of silence may follow.

Prayer
Lord Jesus, your mother and your dearest friend
stayed with you to the bitter end,
yet even while racked with pain you ministered to them:
be with all broken families today
and care for those who long for companionship.
You cared for your loved ones
even in your death-throes:
give us a love for one another
that is stronger even than the fear of death.
To you, Jesus, loving in the face of death,
be honour and glory with the Father and the Holy Spirit,
now and for ever.
All　Amen.

All　Holy God,
holy and strong,
holy and immortal,
have mercy upon us.

Thirteenth Station: Jesus dies on the cross

We adore you, O Christ, and we bless you,
All　because by your holy cross you have redeemed the world.

Reading
A reading from the Gospel according to Mark.

At three o'clock Jesus cried out with a loud voice, 'Eloi, Eloi, lema sabachthani?' which means, 'My God, my God, why have you forsaken me?' When some of the bystanders heard it, they said, 'Listen, he is calling for Elijah.' And someone ran, filled a sponge with sour wine, put it on a stick, and gave it to him to drink, saying, 'Wait, let us see whether Elijah will come to take him down.' Then Jesus gave a loud cry and breathed his last. (*Mark 15:34–7*)

A Reflection, or period of silence may follow.

Prayer
Lord Jesus, you died on the cross
and entered the bleakest of all circumstances:
give courage to those who die at the hands of others.
In death you entered into the darkest place of all:
illumine our darkness with your glorious presence.
To you, Jesus,
your lifeless body hanging on the tree of shame,
be honour and glory with the Father and the Holy Spirit,
now and for ever.
All Amen.

All Holy God,
holy and strong,
holy and immortal,
have mercy upon us.

Fourteenth Station: Jesus laid in the tomb

We adore you, O Christ, and we bless you,
All because by your holy cross you have redeemed the world.

Reading
A reading from the Gospel according to Mark.

Then Joseph bought a linen cloth, and taking down the body, wrapped it in the linen cloth, and laid it in a tomb that had been hewn out of the rock. He then rolled a stone against the door of the tomb. (*Mark 15:46*)

A Reflection, or period of silence may follow.

Prayer
Lord Jesus, Lord of life, you became as nothing for us:
be with those who feel worthless
and as nothing in the world's eyes.
You were laid in a cold, dark tomb
and hidden from sight:
be with all who suffer and die in secret,
hidden from the eyes of the world.
To you, Jesus, your rigid body imprisoned in a tomb,
be honour and glory with the Father and the Holy Spirit,
now and for ever.
All Amen.

All Holy God,
holy and strong,
holy and immortal,
have mercy upon us.

Fifteenth Station: Jesus risen from the dead

We adore you, O Christ, and we bless you,
All because by your holy cross you have redeemed the world.

Reading
A reading from the Gospel according to Mark.

When they looked up, they saw that the stone, which was very large, had already been rolled back. As they entered the tomb, they saw a young man, dressed in a white robe, sitting on the right side; and they were alarmed. But he said to them, 'Do not be alarmed; you are looking for Jesus of Nazareth, who was crucified. He has been raised; he is not here. Look, there is the place they laid him. But go, tell his disciples and Peter that he is going ahead of you to Galilee; there you will see him, just as he told you.' So they went out and fled from the tomb, for terror and amazement had seized them; and they said nothing to anyone, for they were afraid. (*Mark 16:4–8*)

A Reflection, or period of silence may follow.

Prayer
Lord Jesus, you were dead but now you are alive:
transform the torments of this world's sin
that we may see your radiant glory.
You were raised from death to life:
may the power of your resurrection live in us,
that we may be channels
of your true life beyond measure.
To you, Jesus,
who have broken free from the bonds of death,
be honour and glory with the Father and the Holy Spirit,
now and for ever.
All Amen.

All Holy God,
holy and strong,

holy and immortal,
have mercy upon us.

The Conclusion

*A response may be made to the preceding stations. This might
take the form of praise, penitence, intercession or some other
relevant action, accompanied by silence or singing.*

Let us pray for the coming of God's kingdom
in the words our Saviour taught us.

The Lord's Prayer is said.

Most merciful God,
who by the death and resurrection
of your Son Jesus Christ
delivered and saved the world:
grant that by faith in him who suffered on the cross
we may triumph in the power of his victory;
through Jesus Christ your Son our Lord,
who is alive and reigns with you,
in the unity of the Holy Spirit,
one God, now and for ever.

All Amen.

One of the following responsories is used.

You are worthy, O Lamb, for you were slain,
and by your blood you ransomed for God
saints from every tribe and language and nation;
you have made them to be a kingdom and priests
serving our God.

All We adore you, O Christ, and we bless you,
because by your holy cross you have redeemed the
world.

171

To him who loves us
and has freed us from our sins by his blood,
and made us a kingdom of priests
to stand and serve before our God;
All to him who sits upon the throne and to the Lamb
be praise and honour, glory and might,
for ever and ever. Amen.

(or)

All We adore you, O Christ, and we bless you,
because by your holy cross you have redeemed the
world.

Christ was manifested in the body,
vindicated in the spirit,
seen by angels,
proclaimed among the nations,
believed in throughout the world,
glorified in high heaven.
All We adore you, O Christ, and we bless you,
because by your holy cross you have redeemed the
world.

The Lord be with you.
All And also with you.

May God bless us,
that in us may be found love and humility,
obedience and thanksgiving,
discipline, gentleness and peace.
All Amen.

The ministers depart in silence.

The Stations of Joy

The Stations of the Resurrection, or Joy, also known as the *Via Lucis*, the Way of Light, emerged in the last part of the twentieth century, modelled on the older Stations of the Cross, but using the Resurrection experiences from the gospels. There are various arrangements and numbers of stations available. This set comes from the Church of England *Times and Seasons* (p. 444). Not all the stations given here are necessary for use on any one occasion.

The Stations of the Resurrection

I	The earthquake	Matthew 28:2–4
II	Mary Magdalene finds the empty tomb	John 20:1, 2
III	The disciples run to the empty tomb	John 20:3–8
IV	The angel appears to the women	Matthew 28:5–8
V	Jesus meets the women	Matthew 28:9, 10
VI	The road to Emmaus	Luke 24:28–35
VII	Jesus appears to the disciples	Luke 24:36–43 or John 20:19, 20
VIII	Jesus promises the Spirit	Luke 24:44–9
IX	Jesus commissions the disciples	John 20:21–3

X	Jesus breathes the Spirit in the upper room	John 20:22, 23
XI	Jesus reveals himself to Thomas	John 20:24–9
XII	Jesus appears at the lakeside	John 21:9–13
XIII	Jesus confronts Peter	John 21:15–19
XIV	Jesus and the beloved disciple	John 21:20–23
XV	Jesus appears to over five hundred at once	1 Corinthians 15:3–6
XVI	Jesus commissions the disciples	Matthew 28:16–20
XVII	The ascension	Acts 1:3–11
XVIII	Pentecost	Acts 2:1–11
XIX	Jesus appears to Saul (Paul)	Acts 9:1–18 or 1 Corinthians 15:8

The Stations of the Resurrection

The Gathering

At the entrance of the ministers a hymn may be sung.

A minister may say

In the name of the Father,
and of the Son,
and of the Holy Spirit.
All Amen.

Alleluia. Christ is risen.
All He is risen indeed. Alleluia.

Sing for joy, O heavens, and exult, O earth;
break forth, O mountains, into singing!
For the Lord has comforted his people,
and will have compassion on his suffering ones. (*Isaiah 49:13*)

Jesus said, 'This is indeed the will of my Father,
that all who see the Son and believe in him may have
eternal life,
and I will raise them up on the last day.' (*John 6:40*)

The minister introduces the service.

Let us pray.

A brief moment of silence follows.

One of the following Collects is said

Lord of all life and power,
who through the mighty resurrection of your Son
overcame the old order of sin and death
to make all things new in him:
grant that we, being dead to sin
and alive to you in Jesus Christ,
may reign with him in glory;
to whom with you and the Holy Spirit
be praise and honour, glory and might,
now and in all eternity.
All Amen.

(or)

God of glory,
by the raising of your Son
you have broken the chains of death and hell:
fill your Church with faith and hope;
for a new day has dawned
and the way to life stands open
in our Saviour Jesus Christ.
All Amen.

This acclamation may be used

Praise to you, Lord Jesus:
All Dying you destroyed our death,
rising you restored our life:
Lord Jesus, come in glory.

First Station: The earthquake

Jesus is the resurrection and the life.
All Those who believe in him shall never die. Alleluia.

Reading
A reading from the Gospel according to Matthew (28:2–4)

Suddenly there was a great earthquake; for an angel of
the Lord, descending from heaven, came and rolled back
the stone and sat on it. His appearance was like
lightning, and his clothing white as snow. For fear of
him the guards shook and became like dead men.

A Reflection, or period of silence may follow.

Prayer
We praise you and we bless you, our risen Lord Jesus,
King of glory,
for in your resurrection the power of love
breaks open the earth and frees life from death.
As the angel rolled away the stone
from the prison of the tomb,
so release those imprisoned by life's misfortunes.
To you, Lord Jesus,
whose life brings surprises
beyond our wildest expectations,
be honour and glory, now and for ever.
All Amen.

This acclamation may be used.

Praise to you, Lord Jesus:
All Dying you destroyed our death,
rising you restored our life:
Lord Jesus, come in glory.

Second Station: Mary Magdalene finds the empty tomb

Jesus is the resurrection and the life.
All Those who believe in him shall never die. Alleluia.

Reading
A reading from the Gospel according to John (20:1–2)

Early on the first day of the week, while it was still dark, Mary Magdalene came to the tomb and saw that the stone had been removed from the tomb. So she ran and went to Simon Peter and the other disciple, the one whom Jesus loved, and said to them, 'They have taken the Lord out of the tomb, and we do not know where they have laid him.'

A Reflection, or period of silence may follow.

Prayer
We praise you and we bless you, our risen Lord Jesus,
King of glory,
for the love which drew Mary Magdalene to your tomb
to weep over your death.
As you broke into her grief
with your death-shattering life,
so reach into our broken hearts
with your promise of hope.
To you, Lord Jesus,
reaching into the deepest tombs of our despair,
be honour and glory, now and for ever.
All Amen.

This acclamation may be used.

Praise to you, Lord Jesus:
All Dying you destroyed our death,
rising you restored our life:
Lord Jesus, come in glory.

Third Station: The disciples run to the empty tomb

Jesus is the resurrection and the life.
All Those who believe in him shall never die. Alleluia.

Reading
A reading from the Gospel according to John (20:3–8)

Peter and the other disciple set out and went towards
the tomb. The two were running together, but the other
disciple outran Peter and reached the tomb first. He bent
down to look in and saw the linen wrappings lying
there, but he did not go in. Then Simon Peter came,
following him, and went into the tomb. He saw the linen
wrappings lying there, and the cloth that had been on
Jesus' head, not lying with the linen wrappings but
rolled up in a place by itself. Then the other disciple,
who reached the tomb first, also went in, and he saw
and believed.

A Reflection, or period of silence may follow.

Prayer
We praise you and we bless you, our risen Lord Jesus,
King of glory,
for in you our God reveals the awesome power of love
that is stronger even than death.
As in your dying you destroyed death,
so in your rising may we be raised above the trials
and torments of this world's woe.

To you, Lord Jesus,
the fullness of your life revealed in an empty tomb,
be honour and glory, now and for ever.
All Amen

This acclamation may be used.

Praise to you, Lord Jesus:
All Dying you destroyed our death,
rising you restored our life:
Lord Jesus, come in glory.

Fourth Station: The angel appears to the women

Jesus is the resurrection and the life.
All Those who believe in him shall never die. Alleluia.

Reading
A reading from the Gospel according to Matthew (28:5–8)

The angel said to the women, 'Do not be afraid; I know
that you are looking for Jesus who was crucified. He is
not here; for he has been raised, as he said. Come, see
the place where he lay. Then go quickly and tell his
disciples, "He has been raised from the dead, and
indeed he is going ahead of you to Galilee; there you
will see him." This is my message for you.' So they left
the tomb quickly with fear and great joy, and ran to tell
his disciples.

A Reflection, or period of silence may follow.

Prayer
We praise you and we bless you, our risen Lord Jesus,
King of glory,

for your resurrection overturns our expectations of life
and even your closest friends
could not see truth before them.
As the angel helped them to grasp your triumph
and overcome their fear,
so help us to see your hand at work
through the events that overtake us.
To you, Lord Jesus,
whose ways astonish beyond our imagining,
be honour and glory, now and for ever.
All Amen.

This acclamation may be used.

Praise to you, Lord Jesus:
All Dying you destroyed our death,
rising you restored our life:
Lord Jesus, come in glory.

Fifth Station: Jesus meets the women

Jesus is the resurrection and the life.
All Those who believe in him shall never die. Alleluia.

Reading
A reading from the Gospel according to Matthew (28:9–10)

Suddenly Jesus met them and said, 'Greetings!' And
they came to him, took hold of his feet, and worshipped
him. Then Jesus said to them, 'Do not be afraid; go and
tell my brothers to go to Galilee; there they will see me.'

A Reflection, or period of silence may follow.

Prayer
We praise you and we bless you, our risen Lord Jesus,
King of glory,
for your simple word of greeting
made the hearts of the women leap with joy.
Speak your word of love
to those whose hearts are broken,
that they too may hear your loving, beckoning call.
To you, Lord Jesus,
whose call summons us to life in all its fullness,
be honour and glory, now and for ever.
All Amen

This acclamation may be used.

Praise to you, Lord Jesus:
All Dying you destroyed our death,
rising you restored our life:
Lord Jesus, come in glory.

Sixth Station: The road to Emmaus

Jesus is the resurrection and the life.
All Those who believe in him shall never die. Alleluia.

Reading
A reading from the Gospel according to Luke (24:28–35)

As they came near the village to which they were going,
he walked ahead as if he were going on. But they urged
him strongly, saying, 'Stay with us, because it is almost
evening and the day is now nearly over.' So he went in
to stay with them. When he was at the table with them,
he took bread, blessed and broke it, and gave it to them.

Then their eyes were opened, and they recognized him;
and he vanished from their sight. They said to each
other, 'Were not our hearts burning within us while he
was talking to us on the road, while he was opening the
scriptures to us?' That same hour they got up and
returned to Jerusalem; and they found the eleven and
their companions gathered together. They were saying,
'The Lord has risen indeed, and he has appeared to
Simon!' Then they told what had happened on the road,
and how he had been made known to them in the
breaking of the bread.

A Reflection, or period of silence may follow.

Prayer
We praise you and we bless you, our risen Lord Jesus,
King of glory,
for you are with us,
even when our eyes are closed to your companionship.
Walk this day
alongside the disconsolate and the despairing,
open their eyes to your gentle illumination,
and let their hearts burn within them
at your invisible presence.
To you, Lord Jesus,
walking by our side,
be honour and glory, now and for ever.
All Amen

This acclamation may be used.

Praise to you, Lord Jesus:
All Dying you destroyed our death,
rising you restored our life:
Lord Jesus, come in glory.

183

Seventh Station: Jesus appears to the disciples

Jesus is the resurrection and the life.
All Those who believe in him shall never die. Alleluia.

Reading
A reading from the Gospel according to Luke (24:36–43)

While they were talking about this, Jesus himself stood among them and said to them, 'Peace be with you.' They were startled and terrified, and thought that they were seeing a ghost. He said to them, 'Why are you frightened, and why do doubts arise in your hearts? Look at my hands and my feet; see that it is I myself. Touch me and see; for a ghost does not have flesh and bones as you see that I have.' And when he had said this, he showed them his hands and his feet. While in their joy they were disbelieving and still wondering, he said to them, 'Have you anything here to eat?' They gave him a piece of broiled fish, and he took it and ate in their presence.

A Reflection, or period of silence may follow.

Prayer
We praise you and we bless you, our risen Lord Jesus,
King of glory,
for in your birth
you were proclaimed the Prince of Peace,
and in your resurrection you breathe into your people
peace beyond this world's understanding.
Be present, Lord, this day
with those whose lives are disfigured by conflict
and those whose hearts know no peace.

To you, Lord Jesus,
true bringer of the peace of heaven,
be honour and glory, now and for ever.
All Amen

This acclamation may be used.

Praise to you, Lord Jesus:
All Dying you destroyed our death,
rising you restored our life:
Lord Jesus, come in glory.

Eighth Station: Jesus promises the Spirit

Jesus is the resurrection and the life.
All Those who believe in him shall never die. Alleluia.

Reading
A reading from the Gospel according to Luke (24:44–9)

Then he said to them, 'These are my words that I spoke
to you while I was still with you – that everything
written about me in the law of Moses, the prophets, and
the psalms must be fulfilled.' Then he opened their
minds to understand the scriptures, and he said to them,
'Thus it is written, that the Messiah is to suffer and to rise
from the dead on the third day, and that repentance and
forgiveness of sins is to be proclaimed in his name to all
nations, beginning from Jerusalem. You are witnesses of
these things. And see, I am sending upon you what my
Father promised; so stay here in the city until you have
been clothed with power from on high.'

A Reflection, or period of silence may follow.

Prayer
We praise you and we bless you, our risen Lord Jesus,
King of glory,
for you promised that the same power
that was at work when you were raised from the dead
would also be alive in us.
Show your power to those who are powerless;
reveal your love to those who feel unlovely
and through your Spirit enable all your people
to be witnesses of your amazing grace.
To you, Lord Jesus,
daily renewing your people and your creation,
be honour and glory, now and for ever.
All Amen.

This acclamation may be used.

Praise to you, Lord Jesus:
All Dying you destroyed our death,
rising you restored our life:
Lord Jesus, come in glory.

Ninth Station: Jesus commissions the disciples

Jesus is the resurrection and the life.
All Those who believe in him shall never die. Alleluia.

Reading
A reading from the Gospel according to John (20:21–3)

Jesus said to them again, 'Peace be with you. As the
Father has sent me, so I send you.' When he had said
this, he breathed on them and said to them, 'Receive the
Holy Spirit. If you forgive the sins of any, they are

forgiven them; if you retain the sins of any, they are
retained.'

A Reflection, or period of silence may follow.

Prayer
We praise you and we bless you, our risen Lord Jesus,
King of glory,
for as you were sent by the Father, so you send us.
Equip your Church with the gifts to fulfil our calling
that we may love as you loved,
serve as you served,
and willingly follow wherever you lead.
To you, Lord Jesus,
gifting your people,
be honour and glory, now and for ever.
All Amen.

This acclamation may be used.

Praise to you, Lord Jesus:
All Dying you destroyed our death,
rising you restored our life:
Lord Jesus, come in glory.

Tenth Station: Jesus breathes the Spirit in the upper room

Jesus is the resurrection and the life.
All Those who believe in him shall never die. Alleluia.

Reading
A reading from the Gospel according to John (20:22–3)

When Jesus had said this, he breathed on them and said
to them, 'Receive the Holy Spirit. If you forgive the sins

of any, they are forgiven them; if you retain the sins of any, they are retained.'

A Reflection, or period of silence may follow.

Prayer
We praise you and we bless you, our risen Lord Jesus, King of glory,
for you breathed new life into your astonished disciples.
As you turned unutterable grief into unshakeable joy,
so renew and refresh your turbulent world
and establish now your reign of peace.
To you, Lord Jesus,
transforming the pain of death into the fullness of life,
be honour and glory, now and for ever.
All Amen.

This acclamation may be used.

Praise to you, Lord Jesus:
All Dying you destroyed our death,
rising you restored our life:
Lord Jesus, come in glory.

Eleventh Station: Jesus reveals himself to Thomas

Jesus is the resurrection and the life.
All Those who believe in him shall never die. Alleluia.

Reading
A reading from the Gospel according to John (20:24–9)

Thomas (who was called the Twin), one of the twelve, was not with them when Jesus came. So the other disciples told him, 'We have seen the Lord.' But he said to them, 'Unless I see the mark of the nails in his hands, and put my finger in the mark of the nails and my hand in his side, I will not believe.' A week later his disciples were again in the house, and Thomas was with them. Although the doors were shut, Jesus came and stood among them and said, 'Peace be with you.' Then he said to Thomas, 'Put your finger here and see my hands. Reach out your hand and put it in my side. Do not doubt but believe.' Thomas answered him, 'My Lord and my God!' Jesus said to him, 'Have you believed because you have seen me? Blessed are those who have not seen and yet have come to believe.'

A Reflection, or period of silence may follow.

Prayer
We praise you and we bless you, our risen Lord Jesus, King of glory,
for you come to us even in our doubting.
Through the sovereign work of your Spirit,
and the loving hands of your people,
continue to reveal yourself
where doubt is stronger than faith.
To you, Lord Jesus,
whose resurrection body
bears the murderous marks of the cross,
be honour and glory, now and for ever.
All Amen.

This acclamation may be used.

Praise to you, Lord Jesus:
All Dying you destroyed our death,
rising you restored our life:
Lord Jesus, come in glory.

Twelfth Station: Jesus appears at the lakeside

Jesus is the resurrection and the life.
All Those who believe in him shall never die. Alleluia.

Reading
A reading from the Gospel according to John (21:9–13)

When they had gone ashore, they saw a charcoal fire
there, with fish on it, and bread. Jesus said to them,
'Bring some of the fish that you have just caught.' So
Simon Peter went aboard and hauled the net ashore, full
of large fish, a hundred and fifty-three of them; and
though there were so many, the net was not torn. Jesus
said to them, 'Come and have breakfast.' Now none of
the disciples dared to ask him, 'Who are you?' because
they knew it was the Lord. Jesus came and took the
bread and gave it to them, and did the same with the
fish.

A Reflection, or period of silence may follow.

Prayer
We praise you and we bless you, our risen Lord Jesus,
King of glory,
for at the lakeside you showed concern
for the daily needs of your disciples.
As you guided them to fill their nets with fish,
so guide all who are hungry
till their hunger is satisfied in you.
To you, Lord Jesus,
sharing with us the food of faith,
be honour and glory, now and for ever.
All Amen.

This acclamation may be used.

Praise to you, Lord Jesus:
All Dying you destroyed our death,
rising you restored our life:
Lord Jesus, come in glory.

Thirteenth Station: Jesus confronts Peter

Jesus is the resurrection and the life.
All Those who believe in him shall never die. Alleluia.

Reading
A reading from the Gospel according to John (21:15–19)

When they had finished breakfast, Jesus said to Simon
Peter, 'Simon, son of John, do you love me more than
these?' He said to him, 'Yes, Lord; you know that I love
you.' Jesus said to him, 'Feed my lambs.' A second time
he said to him, 'Simon, son of John, do you love me?' He
said to him, 'Yes, Lord; you know that I love you.' Jesus
said to him, 'Tend my sheep.' He said to him the third
time, 'Simon, son of John, do you love me?' Peter felt
hurt because he said to him the third time, 'Do you love
me?' And he said to him, 'Lord, you know everything;
you know that I love you.' Jesus said to him, 'Feed my
sheep. Very truly, I tell you, when you were younger,
you used to fasten your own belt and to go wherever
you wished. But when you grow old, you will stretch
out your hands, and someone else will fasten a belt
around you and take you where you do not wish to go.'
(He said this to indicate the kind of death by which he
would glorify God.) After this he said to him, 'Follow
me.'

A Reflection, or period of silence may follow.

191

Prayer
We praise you and we bless you, our risen Lord Jesus,
King of glory,
for even in the glorious victory of the resurrection
you understood the failure of Peter who denied you.
As you restored him to relationship with you,
remember all who feel downcast
and worthless in this world's eyes
and give them a sense of purpose and value.
To you, Lord Jesus,
loving us despite our denial,
be honour and glory, now and for ever.
All Amen.

This acclamation may be used.

Praise to you, Lord Jesus:
All Dying you destroyed our death,
rising you restored our life:
Lord Jesus, come in glory.

Fourteenth Station: Jesus and the beloved disciple

Jesus is the resurrection and the life.
All Those who believe in him shall never die. Alleluia.

Reading
A reading from the Gospel according to John (21:20–3)

Peter turned and saw the disciple whom Jesus loved
following them; he was the one who had reclined next to
Jesus at the supper and had said, 'Lord, who is it that is
going to betray you?' When Peter saw him, he said to
Jesus, 'Lord, what about him?' Jesus said to him, 'If it is

my will that he remain until I come, what is that to you?
Follow me!' So the rumour spread in the community
that this disciple would not die. Yet Jesus did not say to
him that he would not die, but, 'If it is my will that he
remain until I come, what is that to you?'

A Reflection, or period of silence may follow.

Prayer
We praise you and we bless you, our risen Lord Jesus,
King of glory,
for your single-minded commitment
to your Father's will.
May we be free from distractions of envy or self,
that we might walk the way of the cross
and know the power of your risen life.
To you, Lord Jesus,
treading boldly on the path of suffering,
be honour and glory, now and for ever.
All Amen.

This acclamation may be used.

Praise to you, Lord Jesus:
All Dying you destroyed our death,
rising you restored our life:
Lord Jesus, come in glory.

Fifteenth Station: Jesus appears to over five hundred at once

Jesus is the resurrection and the life.
All Those who believe in him shall never die. Alleluia.

193

Reading
A reading from the First Letter to the Corinthians (15:3–6)

For I handed on to you as of first importance what I in turn had received: that Christ died for our sins in accordance with the scriptures, and that he was buried, and that he was raised on the third day in accordance with the scriptures, and that he appeared to Cephas, then to the twelve. Then he appeared to more than five hundred brothers and sisters at one time, most of whom are still alive, though some have died.

A Reflection, or period of silence may follow.

Prayer
We praise you and we bless you, our risen Lord Jesus,
King of glory,
for your resurrection is a revelation to the whole world.
As you revealed yourself powerfully to so many,
reveal yourself now as the hope for our world.
To you, Lord Jesus,
going beyond the limits of our understanding,
be honour and glory, now and for ever.
All Amen.

This acclamation may be used.

Praise to you, Lord Jesus:
All Dying you destroyed our death,
rising you restored our life:
Lord Jesus, come in glory.

Sixteenth Station: Jesus commissions the disciples on the mountain

Jesus is the resurrection and the life.
All Those who believe in him shall never die. Alleluia.

Reading
A reading from the Gospel according to Matthew (28:16–20)

Now the eleven disciples went to Galilee, to the mountain to which Jesus had directed them. When they saw him, they worshipped him; but some doubted. And Jesus came and said to them, 'All authority in heaven and on earth has been given to me. Go therefore and make disciples of all nations, baptizing them in the name of the Father and of the Son and of the Holy Spirit, and teaching them to obey everything that I have commanded you. And remember, I am with you always, to the end of the age.'

A Reflection, or period of silence may follow.

Prayer
We praise you and we bless you, our risen Lord Jesus,
King of glory,
for you took the risk
of passing your mission to frail disciples.
As you commissioned them to go into all the world,
so may all the world come to you, the King of nations.
To you, Lord Jesus,
with us to the end of the age,
be honour and glory, now and for ever.
All Amen.

This acclamation may be used.

Praise to you, Lord Jesus:
All Dying you destroyed our death,
rising you restored our life:
Lord Jesus, come in glory.

Seventeenth Station: The ascension

Jesus is the resurrection and the life.
All Those who believe in him shall never die. Alleluia.

Reading
A reading from the Acts of the Apostles (1:3–11)

After his suffering he presented himself alive to them by
many convincing proofs, appearing to them over the
course of forty days and speaking about the kingdom of
God. While staying with them, he ordered them not to
leave Jerusalem, but to wait there for the promise of the
Father. 'This', he said, 'is what you have heard from me;
for John baptized with water, but you will be baptized
with the Holy Spirit not many days from now.' So when
they had come together, they asked him, 'Lord, is this
the time when you will restore the kingdom to Israel?'
He replied, 'It is not for you to know the times or
periods that the Father has set by his own authority. But
you will receive power when the Holy Spirit has come
upon you; and you will be my witnesses in Jerusalem, in
all Judea and Samaria, and to the ends of the earth.'
When he had said this, as they were watching, he was
lifted up, and a cloud took him out of their sight.
While he was going and they were gazing up towards
heaven, suddenly two men in white robes stood by them.

They said, 'Men of Galilee, why do you stand looking
up towards heaven? This Jesus, who has been taken up
from you into heaven, will come in the same way as you
saw him go into heaven.'

A Reflection, or period of silence may follow.

Prayer
We praise you and we bless you, our risen Lord Jesus,
King of glory,
for in your ascension
you are crowned King of kings and Lord of lords.
As we worship you on your heavenly throne,
prepare our hearts for the coming of your Spirit.
To you, Lord Jesus,
who will come back in the same way
you went up into heaven,
be honour and glory, now and for ever.
All Amen.

This acclamation may be used.

Praise to you, Lord Jesus:
All Dying you destroyed our death,
rising you restored our life:
Lord Jesus, come in glory.

Eighteenth Station: Pentecost

Jesus is the resurrection and the life.
All Those who believe in him shall never die. Alleluia.

Reading
A reading from the Acts of the Apostles (2:1–11)

When the day of Pentecost had come, they were all together in one place. And suddenly from heaven there came a sound like the rush of a violent wind, and it filled the entire house where they were sitting. Divided tongues, as of fire, appeared among them, and a tongue rested on each of them. All of them were filled with the Holy Spirit and began to speak in other languages, as the Spirit gave them ability. Now there were devout Jews from every nation under heaven living in Jerusalem. And at this sound the crowd gathered and was bewildered, because each one heard them speaking in the native language of each. Amazed and astonished, they asked, 'Are not all these who are speaking Galileans? And how is it that we hear, each of us, in our own native language? Parthians, Medes, Elamites, and residents of Mesopotamia, Judea and Cappadocia, Pontus and Asia, Phrygia and Pamphylia, Egypt and the parts of Libya belonging to Cyrene, and visitors from Rome, both Jews and proselytes, Cretans and Arabs – in our own languages we hear them speaking about God's deeds of power.'

A Reflection, or period of silence may follow.

Prayer
We praise you and we bless you, our risen Lord Jesus, King of glory,
for you promised that your disciples
would be baptized with the Holy Spirit
and now we see the fulfilment of your promise.
Fill us afresh with your Spirit today,
revive your Church,
and renew the face of the earth.
To you, Lord Jesus,

giving to your people the greatest gift of all,
be honour and glory, now and for ever.
All Amen.

This acclamation may be used.

Praise to you, Lord Jesus:
All Dying you destroyed our death,
rising you restored our life:
Lord Jesus, come in glory.

Nineteenth Station: Jesus appears to Saul (Paul)

Jesus is the resurrection and the life.
All Those who believe in him shall never die. Alleluia.

Reading
A reading from the Acts of the Apostles (9:1–18)

Saul, still breathing threats and murder against the
disciples of the Lord, went to the high priest and asked
him for letters to the synagogues at Damascus, so that if
he found any who belonged to the Way, men or women,
he might bring them bound to Jerusalem. Now as he
was going along and approaching Damascus, suddenly
a light from heaven flashed around him. He fell to the
ground and heard a voice saying to him, 'Saul, Saul,
why do you persecute me?' He asked, 'Who are you,
Lord?' The reply came, 'I am Jesus, whom you are
persecuting. But get up and enter the city, and you will
be told what you are to do.' The men who were
travelling with him stood speechless because they heard
the voice but saw no one. Saul got up from the ground,
and though his eyes were open, he could see nothing; so

they led him by the hand and brought him into
Damascus. For three days he was without sight, and
neither ate nor drank. Now there was a disciple in
Damascus named Ananias. The Lord said to him in a
vision, 'Ananias.' He answered, 'Here I am, Lord.' The
Lord said to him, 'Get up and go to the street called
Straight, and at the house of Judas look for a man of
Tarsus named Saul. At this moment he is praying, and
he has seen in a vision a man named Ananias come in
and lay his hands on him so that he might regain his
sight.' But Ananias answered, 'Lord, I have heard from
many about this man, how much evil he has done to
your saints in Jerusalem; and here he has authority from
the chief priests to bind all who invoke your name.' But
the Lord said to him, 'Go, for he is an instrument whom
I have chosen to bring my name before Gentiles and
kings and before the people of Israel; I myself will show
him how much he must suffer for the sake of my name.'
So Ananias went and entered the house. He laid his
hands on Saul and said, 'Brother Saul, the Lord Jesus,
who appeared to you on your way here, has sent me so
that you may regain your sight and be filled with the
Holy Spirit.'
And immediately something like scales fell from his
eyes, and his sight was restored. Then he got up and
was baptized.

A Reflection, or period of silence may follow.

Prayer
We praise you and we bless you, our risen Lord Jesus,
King of glory,
for you transformed the murderous Saul
into the great apostle, Paul.

As you revealed yourself to him
on the road to Damascus,
reveal yourself afresh
to your people journeying through this life.
To you, Lord Jesus,
who can fill even the emptiest of lives,
be honour and glory, now and for ever.
All Amen.

This acclamation may be used.

Praise to you, Lord Jesus:
All Dying you destroyed our death,
rising you restored our life:
Lord Jesus, come in glory.

The Conclusion

A response may be made to the preceding stations. This might take the form of praise, penitence, intercession or some other relevant action, accompanied by silence or singing.

Let us pray for the coming of God's kingdom
in the words our Saviour taught us.

The Lord's Prayer is said.

Almighty God,
whose Son Jesus Christ is the resurrection and the life:
raise us, who trust in him,
from the death of sin to the life of righteousness,
that we may seek those things that are above
where he reigns with you
in the unity of the Holy Spirit,
one God, now and for ever.
All Amen

Alleluia. Christ is risen.
All He is risen indeed. Alleluia.

Praise the God and Father of our Lord Jesus Christ.
All He has given us new life and hope.
He has raised Jesus from the dead.

God has claimed us as his own.
All He has brought us out of darkness.
He has made us light to the world.

Alleluia. Christ is risen.
All He is risen indeed. Alleluia.

God the Father,
by whose glory Christ was raised from the dead,
strengthen you to walk with him in his risen life;
and the blessing of God almighty,
the Father, the Son, and the Holy Spirit,
be among you and remain with you always.
All Amen.

These or other suitable words introduce the Peace.

The risen Christ came and stood among his disciples
and said 'Peace be with you'.
Then were they glad to see the Lord. Alleluia.
The peace of the risen Lord be always with you
All and also with you.

Let us offer one another a sign of peace.

All may exchange a sign of peace.

Stations of Healing

The Stations of Healing may be performed for people we know who are ill, or for ourselves. We can also perform them for everyone and anyone in the world who is sick, suffering, or in any kind of trouble. There are fifteen readings for stations here, and you are free to use as many as you see fit, or even to repeat them if you wish. Keep the person(s) in your mind's eye while you walk and pray. If you are praying for people you don't know, remember the times when you had trouble and suffering in your own life, and the healing you needed at that time, and send out that healing to them from your heart and in your prayers.

The practice of lovingkindness meditation would be very suitable here, and could be performed between the stations, as you walk along. See Chapter Seven for details of how to practise it. You could also do Lectio Divina with a phrase from the reading to use between the stations.

This is written to be used in a group. On your own, just say all the words.

The Beginning

> In the name of the Father,
> and of the Son,
> and of the Holy Spirit.
>
> The Lord be with you
> *All* And also with you.

Jesus, as a mother you gather your people to you;
you are gentle with us as a mother to her children.
You comfort us in sorrow and bind up our wounds;
in sickness you nurse us and with pure milk you feed us.
(*St Anselm*)

O Lord, listen to my prayer and let my cry for help reach
you.
Do not hide your face from me in the day of my distress.
Turn your ear towards me and answer quickly when I
call. (*Psalm 101*)

Are any among you suffering? They should pray. Are
any cheerful? They should sing songs of praise. Are any
among you sick? They should call for the elders of the
church and have them pray over them, anointing them
with oil in the name of the Lord. The prayer of faith will
save the sick, and the Lord will raise them up; and
anyone who has committed sins will be forgiven.
Therefore confess your sins to one another, and pray for
one another, so that you may be healed. The prayer of
the righteous is powerful and effective. (*James 5: 13–16*)

God the Father, your will for all people is health and
salvation.
All We praise and bless you, Lord.

God the Son, you came that we might have life,
and might have it more abundantly.
All We praise and bless you, Lord.

God the Holy Spirit, you make our bodies
the temple of your presence.
All We praise and bless you, Lord.

Holy Trinity, one God, in you we live and move and
have our being.
All We praise and bless you, Lord.

Lord, grant your healing grace to all
who are sick, injured or disabled,
all who suffer or are in any trouble,
that they may be made whole.
All Hear us, Lord of life. (*Book of Common Prayer*, 2004, p. 461)

Let us be silent before God.

A period of silence follows.

O Lord our God,
accept the fervent prayers of your people;
in the multitude of your mercies look with compassion
upon us and all who turn to you for help;
for you are gracious, O lover of souls,
and to you we give glory, Father, Son, and Holy Spirit,
now and for ever. Amen. (*BCP*, 2004, p. 461)

Our help is in the name of the Lord
All who has made heaven and earth.

Blessed be the name of the Lord:
All now and for ever. Amen.

Let us proceed in peace.

Station Format

Jesus, as a mother you gather your people to you;
you are gentle with us as a mother to her children.
You comfort us in sorrow and bind up our wounds;
in sickness you nurse us and with pure milk you feed us.

A Reading from the selection below.

A Reflection, or period of silence may follow.

Prayer
O Lord our God,
accept the fervent prayers of your people;
in the multitude of your mercies look with compassion
upon us and all who turn to you for help;
for you are gracious, O lover of souls,
and to you we give glory, Father, Son and Holy Spirit,
now and forever. Amen. (*BCP*, 2004, p. 460)

Our help is in the name of the Lord
All who has made heaven and earth.

Blessed be the name of the Lord:
All now and for ever. Amen.

Conclusion

Response
This can be in the form of silent meditation, prayers or
intercessions, personal or collective, and can take the form of
praise, penitence, intercession or thanks.

We pray for the coming of God's kingdom
in the words our Saviour taught us:
Our Father …

Final Prayer
Heavenly Father,
you anointed your Son Jesus Christ
with the Holy Spirit and with power
to bring to us the blessings of your kingdom.
Anoint your Church with the same Holy Spirit,
that we who share in his suffering and victory
may bear witness to the gospel of salvation;
through Jesus Christ, your Son our Lord,
who is alive and reigns with you
in the unity of the Holy Spirit,
one God, now and for ever. Amen. (*BCP*, 2004, p. 458)

Blessing
May Christ,
who out of defeat brings a new hope and a new future,
fill you/us with his new life;
and the blessing of God almighty,
the Father, the Son and the Holy Spirit,
be with you/us and remain with you/us for ever.
Amen.

The Peace
The presiding minister introduces the Peace with these or
other suitable words.

Jesus says:
'Peace I leave with you. My peace I give to you.
Not as the world gives, give I unto you.
Do not let your hearts be troubled,
neither let them be afraid.'
The peace of the Lord be always with you.
All And always with you.

Let us offer one another a sign of peace.

Suggested Readings

Lamentations 3:17–24

My soul is bereft of peace; I have forgotten what happiness is; so I say, 'Gone is my glory, and all that I had hoped for from the Lord.' The thought of my affliction and my homelessness is wormwood and gall! My soul continually thinks of it and is bowed down within me. But this I call to mind, and therefore I have hope: The steadfast love of the Lord never ceases, his mercies never come to an end; they are new every morning; great is your faithfulness. 'The Lord is my portion,' says my soul, 'therefore I will hope in him.'

Mark 6:54–6

When they got out of the boat, people at once recognised him, and rushed about that whole region and began to bring the sick on mats to wherever they heard he was. And wherever he went, into villages or cities or farms, they laid the sick in the marketplaces, and begged him that they might touch even the fringe of his cloak; and all who touched it were healed.

Mark 5, 36b–43

Jesus said to the leader of the synagogue, 'Do not fear, only believe.' He allowed no one to follow him except Peter, James, and John, the brother of James. When they came to the house of the leader of the synagogue, he saw a commotion, people weeping and wailing loudly. When he had entered, he said to them, 'Why do you make a commotion and weep? The child is not dead but sleeping.' And they laughed at him. Then he put them all outside, and took the child's father and mother and those who were with him, and went in where the child was. He took her by the hand and said to her, 'Talitha cum,' which means, 'Little girl, get up!' And immediately the girl got up and began to walk about (she was twelve years of age). At this they were overcome with amazement. He strictly ordered them that no one should know this, and told them to give her something to eat.

Matthew 28:5–10
But the angel said to the women, 'Do not be afraid; I know that you are looking for Jesus who was crucified. He is not here; for he has been raised, as he said. Come, see the place where he lay. Then go quickly and tell his disciples, "He has been raised from the dead, and indeed he is going ahead of you to Galilee; there you will see him." This is my message for you.' So they left the tomb quickly with fear and great joy, and ran to tell his disciples. Suddenly Jesus met them and said, 'Greetings!' And they came to him, took hold of his feet, and worshipped him. Then Jesus said to them, 'Do not be afraid; go and tell my brothers to go to Galilee; there they will see me.'

Mark 14:32–8
They went to a place called Gethsemane; and he said to his disciples, 'Sit here while I pray.' He took with him Peter and James and John, and began to be distressed and agitated. And he said to them, 'I am deeply grieved, even to death; remain here, and keep awake.' And going a little farther, he threw himself on the ground and prayed that, if it were possible, the hour might pass from him. He said, 'Abba, Father, for you all things are

possible; remove this cup from me; yet, not what I want, but what you want.' He came and found them sleeping; and he said to Peter, 'Simon, are you asleep? Could you not keep awake one hour? Keep awake and pray that you may not come into the time of trial; the spirit indeed is willing, but the flesh is weak.'

Luke 17:11–19
On the way to Jerusalem Jesus was going through the region between Samaria and Galilee. As he entered a village, ten lepers approached him. Keeping their distance, they called out, saying, 'Jesus, Master, have mercy on us!' When he saw them, he said to them, 'Go and show yourselves to the priests.' And as they went, they were made clean. Then one of them, when he saw that he was healed, turned back, praising God with a loud voice. He prostrated himself at Jesus' feet and thanked him. And he was a Samaritan. Then Jesus asked, 'Were not ten made clean? But the other nine, where are they? Was none of them found to return and give praise to God except this foreigner?' Then he said to him, 'Get up and go on your way; your faith has made you well.'

Mark 5
Now there was a woman who had been suffering from haemorrhages for twelve years. She had endured much under many physicians, and had spent all that she had; and she was no better, but rather grew worse. She had heard about Jesus, and came up behind him in the crowd and touched his cloak, for she said, 'If I but touch his clothes, I will be made well.' Immediately her haemorrhage stopped; and she felt in her body that she was healed of her disease. Immediately aware that

power had gone forth from him, Jesus turned about in the crowd and said, 'Who touched my clothes?' And his disciples said to him, 'You see the crowd pressing in on you; how can you say, "Who touched me?"' He looked all around to see who had done it. But the woman, knowing what had happened to her, came in fear and trembling, fell down before him, and told him the whole truth. He said to her, 'Daughter, your faith has made you well; go in peace, and be healed of your disease.'

Mark 1
They went to Capernaum; and when the sabbath came, he entered the synagogue and taught. They were astounded at his teaching, for he taught them as one having authority, and not as the scribes. Just then there was in their synagogue a man with an unclean spirit, and he cried out, 'What have you to do with us, Jesus of Nazareth? Have you come to destroy us? I know who you are, the Holy One of God.' But Jesus rebuked him, saying, 'Be silent, and come out of him!' And the unclean spirit, convulsing him and crying with a loud voice, came out of him. They were all amazed, and they kept on asking one another, 'What is this? A new teaching – with authority! He commands even the unclean spirits, and they obey him.' At once his fame began to spread throughout the surrounding region of Galilee.

2 Corinthians 12:7b–10
To keep me from being too elated, a thorn was given me in the flesh, a messenger of Satan to torment me, to keep me from being too elated. Three times I appealed to the Lord about this, that it would leave me, but he said to

me, 'My grace is sufficient for you, for power is made perfect in weakness.' So, I will boast all the more gladly of my weaknesses, so that the power of Christ may dwell in me. Therefore I am content with weaknesses, insults, hardships, persecutions, and calamities for the sake of Christ; for whenever I am weak, then I am strong.

Psalm 23
1 The Lord is my shepherd, I shall not want.
2 He makes me lie down in green pastures;
he leads me beside still waters;
3 he restores my soul.
He leads me in right paths
for his name's sake.
4 Even though I walk through the darkest valley,
I fear no evil;
for you are with me;
your rod and your staff –
they comfort me.
5 You prepare a table before me
in the presence of my enemies;
you anoint my head with oil;
my cup overflows.
6 Surely goodness and mercy shall follow me
all the days of my life,
and I shall dwell in the house of the Lord
my whole life long.

Psalm 27:1–10, 13–14
1 The Lord is my light and my salvation;
whom shall I fear?
The Lord is the stronghold of my life;
of whom shall I be afraid?

2 When evildoers assail me
to devour my flesh –
my adversaries and foes –
they shall stumble and fall.
3 Though an army encamp against me,
my heart shall not fear;
though war rise up against me,
yet I will be confident.
4 One thing I asked of the Lord,
that will I seek after:
to live in the house of the Lord
all the days of my life,
to behold the beauty of the Lord,
and to inquire in his temple.
5 For he will hide me in his shelter
in the day of trouble;
he will conceal me under the cover of his tent;
he will set me high on a rock.
6 Now my head is lifted up
above my enemies all around me,
and I will offer in his tent
sacrifices with shouts of joy;
I will sing and make melody to the Lord.
7 Hear, O Lord, when I cry aloud,
be gracious to me and answer me!
8 'Come,' my heart says, 'seek his face!'
Your face, Lord, do I seek.
9 Do not hide your face from me.
Do not turn your servant away in anger,
you who have been my help.
Do not cast me off, do not forsake me,
O God of my salvation!

10 If my father and mother forsake me,
the Lord will take me up.

13 I believe that I shall see the goodness of the Lord
in the land of the living.
14 Wait for the Lord;
be strong, and let your heart take courage;
wait for the Lord!

Psalm 103:1–5, 8–14
1 Bless the Lord, O my soul,
and all that is within me,
bless his holy name.
2 Bless the Lord, O my soul,
and do not forget all his benefits –
3 who forgives all your iniquity,
who heals all your diseases,
4 who redeems your life from the Pit,
who crowns you with steadfast love and mercy,
5 who satisfies you with good as long as you live
so that your youth is renewed like the eagle's.

8 The Lord is merciful and gracious,
slow to anger and abounding in steadfast love.
9 He will not always accuse,
nor will he keep his anger forever.
10 He does not deal with us according to our sins,
nor repay us according to our iniquities.
11 For as the heavens are high above the earth,
so great is his steadfast love toward those who fear him;
12 as far as the east is from the west,
so far he removes our transgressions from us.
13 As a father has compassion for his children,
so the Lord has compassion for those who fear him.

14 For he knows how we were made;
he remembers that we are dust.

Psalm 139:1–18
1 O Lord, you have searched me and known me.
2 You know when I sit down and when I rise up;
you discern my thoughts from far away.
3 You search out my path and my lying down,
and are acquainted with all my ways.
4 Even before a word is on my tongue,
O Lord, you know it completely.
5 You hem me in, behind and before,
and lay your hand upon me.
6 Such knowledge is too wonderful for me;
it is so high that I cannot attain it.
7 Where can I go from your spirit?
Or where can I flee from your presence?
8 If I ascend to heaven, you are there;
if I make my bed in Sheol, you are there.
9 If I take the wings of the morning
and settle at the farthest limits of the sea,
10 even there your hand shall lead me,
and your right hand shall hold me fast.
11 If I say, 'Surely the darkness shall cover me,
and the light around me become night,'
12 even the darkness is not dark to you;
the night is as bright as the day,
for darkness is as light to you.
13 For it was you who formed my inward parts;
you knit me together in my mother's womb.
14 I praise you, for I am fearfully and wonderfully made.
Wonderful are your works;
that I know very well.

15 My frame was not hidden from you,
when I was being made in secret,
intricately woven in the depths of the earth.
16 Your eyes beheld my unformed substance.
In your book were written
all the days that were formed for me,
when none of them as yet existed.
17 How weighty to me are your thoughts, O God!
How vast is the sum of them!
18 I try to count them – they are more than the sand;
I come to the end – I am still with you.

Psalm 131
A prayer of humble trust
1 O Lord, my heart is not lifted up,
my eyes are not raised too high;
I do not occupy myself with things
too great and too marvellous for me.
2 But I have calmed and quieted my soul,
like a weaned child with its mother;
my soul is like the weaned child that is with me.
3 O Israel, hope in the Lord
from this time on and forevermore.

Psalm 42:1–9, 11
1 As a deer longs for flowing streams,
so my soul longs for you, O God.
2 My soul thirsts for God,
for the living God.
When shall I come and behold
the face of God?
3 My tears have been my food
day and night,

while people say to me continually,
'Where is your God?'
4 These things I remember,
as I pour out my soul:
how I went with the throng,
and led them in procession to the house of God,
with glad shouts and songs of thanksgiving,
a multitude keeping festival.
5 Why are you cast down, O my soul,
and why are you disquieted within me?
Hope in God; for I shall again praise him,
my help
6 and my God.
My soul is cast down within me;
therefore I remember you
from the land of Jordan and of Hermon,
from Mount Mizar.
7 Deep calls to deep
at the thunder of your cataracts;
all your waves and your billows
have gone over me.
8 By day the Lord commands his steadfast love,
and at night his song is with me,
a prayer to the God of my life.
9 I say to God, my rock,
'Why have you forgotten me?
Why must I walk about mournfully
because the enemy oppresses me?'

11 Why are you cast down, O my soul,
and why are you disquieted within me?
Hope in God; for I shall again praise him,
my help and my God.

The Stations of the Teaching of Jesus Christ

There are three elements (at least!) to Jesus Christ. The traditional emphasis is on his salvific death and on his resurrection, but his life and the teaching embodied in it are also important. We have only one extended passage of Christ's teaching, in the Sermon on the Mount in Matthew's Gospel, with a shorter version in Luke's. Of course the stories *about* Christ in the gospels aren't there as history or biography, primarily, they are there as examples of Christ's teaching as well. His entire life can be considered a teaching.

These stations are from Matthew's Sermon on the Mount. They are not the entirety of Jesus' teachings, but they give the core and thrust. Meditation on them can only be a good thing.

The Beginning

The ministers enter in silence.

In the name of the Father,
and of the Son,
and of the Holy Spirit.
All Amen.

The Lord be with you.
All And also with you.

He said to them, 'You shall love the Lord your God with all your heart, and with all your soul, and with all your mind.' This is the greatest and first commandment. And a second is like it: 'You shall love your neighbour as yourself.' On these two commandments hang all the law and the prophets. (*Matthew 22:37–9*)

Come to me, all you that are weary and are carrying heavy burdens, and I will give you rest. Take my yoke upon you, and learn from me; for I am gentle and humble in heart, and you will find rest for your souls. For my yoke is easy, and my burden is light. (*Matthew 11:28–30*)

I will meditate on your precepts,
and fix my eyes on your ways.
All Open my eyes, so that I may behold
wondrous things out of your law. (*Psalm 119:15, 18*)

Collect

Let us be silent before God.

A brief moment of silence follows.

God of all truth,
let us hear your voice in our hearts,
that we may learn and believe
that the law which binds all law is that of love,
and may walk in ways of wisdom and peace all our days,
to the glory of your Son, Jesus Christ our Lord.
All Amen.

Lord, have mercy.
All Lord have mercy.

Christ have mercy.
All Christ have mercy.

Lord, have mercy.
All Lord have mercy.

Make your ways known upon earth, Lord God,
All your saving power among all peoples.

Renew us in holiness
All and help us to serve you with joy.

Guide the leaders of this and every nation,
All that justice may prevail throughout the world.

Let not the needy be forgotten,
All nor the hope of the poor be taken away.

Make us instruments of your peace
All and let your glory be over all the earth.
(*New Patterns for Worship, 186*)

Let us proceed in peace.

Station Format

I will meditate on your precepts,
and fix my eyes on your ways.
All Open my eyes, so that I may behold
wondrous things out of your law. (*Psalm 119:15, 18*)

A Reading from the series below.

A Reflection, or period of silence may follow.

Prayer
Lord, you are the source of all wisdom;
allow us to hear your teaching,
so that your words may bring light to our minds,
and guide our feet on the path of life.

Open our hearts and fill them
with enough love for God,
neighbours and enemies,
to your honour and glory.
All Amen.

Let my cry come before you, O Lord;
All Give me understanding according to your word.

(*Psalm 119:169*)

Conclusion

Response
This can be in the form of silent meditation, prayers or intercessions, personal or collective, and can take the form of praise, penitence, intercession or thanks.

We pray for the coming of God's kingdom
in the words our Saviour taught us:
Our Father…

Final Prayer
Lord, you have taught us
that all our doings without love are worth nothing:
send your Holy Spirit
and pour into our hearts
that most excellent gift of love,
the true bond of peace
and of all virtues,
without which whoever lives
is counted dead before you.
Grant this for the sake of your only Son,
Jesus Christ our Lord.
Amen. (*Book of Common Prayer, 2004, p. 283*)

Blessing
May the teachings of Christ
open our eyes and ears to the love of God in the world.
And the blessing of God almighty,
Father, Son and Holy Spirit,
be with you and remain with you always.
All Amen.

The Peace
Jesus said, 'I give you a new commandment, that you
love one another. Just as I have loved you, you also
should love one another. By this everyone will know
that you are my disciples, if you have love for one
another. (*John 13:34–5*)

The peace of the Lord be always with you:
All And always with you.

Let us offer one another a sign of peace.

First Station: The Beatitudes
When Jesus saw the crowds, he went up the mountain;
and after he sat down, his disciples came to him. Then
he began to speak, and taught them, saying: 'Blessed are
the poor in spirit, for theirs is the kingdom of heaven.
Blessed are those who mourn, for they will be comforted.
Blessed are the meek, for they will inherit the earth.
Blessed are those who hunger and thirst for
righteousness, for they will be filled. Blessed are the
merciful, for they will receive mercy. Blessed are the
pure in heart, for they will see God. Blessed are the
peacemakers, for they will be called children of God.
Blessed are those who are persecuted for righteousness'

sake, for theirs is the kingdom of heaven. Blessed are you when people revile you and persecute you and utter all kinds of evil against you falsely on my account. Rejoice and be glad, for your reward is great in heaven, for in the same way they persecuted the prophets who were before you.' (*Matthew 5:1–12*)

Second Station: The disciple in the world

'You are the salt of the earth; but if salt has lost its taste, how can its saltiness be restored? It is no longer good for anything, but is thrown out and trampled under foot. You are the light of the world. A city built on a hill cannot be hid. No one after lighting a lamp puts it under the bushel basket, but on the lampstand, and it gives light to all in the house. In the same way, let your light shine before others, so that they may see your good works and give glory to your Father in heaven.' (*Matthew 5:13–16*)

Third Station: Jesus and the law

'For I tell you, unless your righteousness exceeds that of the scribes and Pharisees, you will never enter the kingdom of heaven. You have heard that it was said to those of ancient times, "You shall not murder"; and "whoever murders shall be liable to judgment." But I say to you that if you are angry with a brother or sister, you will be liable to judgment; and if you insult a brother or sister, you will be liable to the council; and if you say, "You fool," you will be liable to the hell of fire. So when you are offering your gift at the altar, if you remember that your brother or sister has something against you, leave your gift there before the altar and go; first be reconciled to your brother or sister, and then come and offer your gift. Come to terms quickly with your accuser while you are on the way to court with him, or your accuser may hand you over to the judge, and the judge to the guard, and you will be thrown into prison. Truly I tell you, you will never get out until you have paid the last penny.' (*Matthew 5:20–6*)

Fourth Station: Adultery

'You have heard that it was said, "You shall not commit adultery." But I say to you that everyone who looks at a woman with lust has already committed adultery with her in his heart. If your right eye causes you to sin, tear it out and throw it away; it is better for you to lose one of your members than for your whole body to be thrown into hell. And if your right hand causes you to sin, cut it off and throw it away; it is better for you to lose one of your members than for your whole body to go into hell.

'It was also said, "Whoever divorces his wife, let him give her a certificate of divorce." But I say to you that anyone who divorces his wife, except on the ground of unchastity, causes her to commit adultery; and whoever marries a divorced woman commits adultery.' (*Matthew 5:27–32*)

Fifth Station: Oaths

'Again, you have heard that it was said to those of ancient times, "You shall not swear falsely, but carry out the vows you have made to the Lord." But I say to you, Do not swear at all, either by heaven, for it is the throne of God, or by the earth, for it is his footstool, or by

Jerusalem, for it is the city of the great King. And do not swear by your head, for you cannot make one hair white or black. Let your word be "Yes, Yes" or "No, No"; anything more than this comes from the evil one.' (*Matthew 5:33–7*)

Sixth Station: Do not resist an evildoer

'You have heard that it was said, "An eye for an eye and a tooth for a tooth." But I say to you, Do not resist an evildoer. But if anyone strikes you on the right cheek, turn the other also; and if anyone wants to sue you and take your coat, give your cloak as well; and if anyone forces you to go one mile, go also the second mile. Give to everyone who begs from you, and do not refuse anyone who wants to borrow from you.' (*Matthew 5:38–42*)

Seventh Station: Love and wholeness

'You have heard that it was said, "You shall love your neighbour and hate your enemy." But I say to you, Love your enemies and pray for those who persecute you, so that you may be children of your Father in heaven; for he makes his sun rise on the evil and on the good, and sends rain on the righteous and on the unrighteous. For if you love those who love you, what reward do you have? Do not even the tax collectors do the same? And if you greet only your brothers and sisters, what more are you doing than others? Do not even the Gentiles do the same? Be perfect, therefore, as your heavenly Father is perfect.' (*Matthew 5:43–8*)

Eighth Station: On justice and prayer

'Beware of practicing your piety before others in order to be seen by them; for then you have no reward from your Father in heaven.

'So whenever you give alms, do not sound a trumpet before you, as the hypocrites do in the synagogues and in the streets, so that they may be praised by others. Truly I tell you, they have received their reward. But when you give alms, do not let your left hand know what your right hand is doing, so that your alms may be done in secret; and your Father who sees in secret will reward you.

'And whenever you pray, do not be like the hypocrites; for they love to stand and pray in the synagogues and at the street corners, so that they may be seen by others. Truly I tell you, they have received their reward. But whenever you pray, go into your room and shut the door and pray to your Father who is in secret; and your Father who sees in secret will reward you.

'When you are praying, do not heap up empty phrases as the Gentiles do; for they think that they will be heard because of their many words. Do not be like them, for your Father knows what you need before you ask him.

'Pray then in this way: Our Father in heaven, hallowed be your name. Your kingdom come. Your will be done, on earth as it is in heaven. Give us this day our daily bread. And forgive us our debts, as we also have forgiven our debtors. And do not bring us to the time of trial, but rescue us from the evil one.

'For if you forgive others their trespasses, your heavenly Father will also forgive you; but if you do not forgive others, neither will your Father forgive your trespasses.' (*Matthew 6:1–15*)

Ninth Station: Fasting

'And whenever you fast, do not look dismal, like the hypocrites, for they disfigure their faces so as to show others that they are fasting. Truly I tell you, they have received their reward. But when you fast, put oil on your head and wash your face, so that your fasting may be seen not by others but by your Father who is in secret; and your Father who sees in secret will reward you.' (*Matthew 6:16–18*)

Tenth Station: Religion and possessions

'Do not store up for yourselves treasures on earth, where moth and rust consume and where thieves break in and steal; but store up for yourselves treasures in heaven, where neither moth nor rust consumes and where thieves do not break in and steal. For where your treasure is, there your heart will be also.

'The eye is the lamp of the body. So, if your eye is healthy, your whole body will be full of light; but if your eye is unhealthy, your whole body will be full of darkness. If then the light in you is darkness, how great is the darkness!

'No one can serve two masters; for a slave will either hate the one and love the other, or be devoted to the one and despise the other. You cannot serve God and wealth.' (*Matthew 6:19–24*)

Eleventh Station: Do not worry

'Therefore I tell you, do not worry about your life, what you will eat or what you will drink, or about your body, what you will wear. Is not life more than food, and the body more than clothing? Look at the birds of the air; they neither sow nor reap nor gather into barns, and yet your heavenly Father feeds them. Are you not of more value than they? And can any of you by worrying add a single hour to your span of life? And why do you worry about clothing? Consider the lilies of the field, how they grow; they neither toil nor spin, yet I tell you, even Solomon in all his glory was not clothed like one of these. But if God so clothes the grass of the field, which is alive today and tomorrow is thrown into the oven, will he not much more clothe you – you of little faith? Therefore do not worry, saying, "What will we eat?" or "What will we drink?" or "What will we wear?" For it is the Gentiles who strive for all these things; and indeed your heavenly Father knows that you need all these things. But strive first for the kingdom of God and his righteousness, and all these things will be given to you as well.

'So do not worry about tomorrow, for tomorrow will bring worries of its own. Today's trouble is enough for today.' (*Matthew 6:25–34*)

Twelfth Station: Making judgments within the community

'Do not judge, so that you may not be judged. For with the judgment you make you will be judged, and the measure you give will be the measure you get. Why do you see the speck in your neighbour's eye, but do not notice the log in your own eye? Or how can you say to

your neighbour, "Let me take the speck out of your eye,"
while the log is in your own eye? You hypocrite, first
take the log out of your own eye, and then you will see
clearly to take the speck out of your neighbour's eye.

'Do not give what is holy to dogs; and do not throw
your pearls before swine, or they will trample them
under foot and turn and maul you.' (*Matthew 7:1–6*)

Thirteenth Station: Ask. Seek. Knock

'Ask, and it will be given you; search, and you will find;
knock, and the door will be opened for you. For
everyone who asks receives, and everyone who searches
finds, and for everyone who knocks, the door will be
opened. Is there anyone among you who, if your child
asks for bread, will give a stone? Or if the child asks for
a fish, will give a snake? If you then, who are evil, know
how to give good gifts to your children, how much more
will your Father in heaven give good things to those
who ask him!' (*Matthew 7:7–11*)

Fourteenth Station: Bearing fruit

'In everything do to others as you would have them do
to you; for this is the law and the prophets.

'Enter through the narrow gate; for the gate is wide
and the road is easy that leads to destruction, and there
are many who take it. For the gate is narrow and the
road is hard that leads to life, and there are few who find
it.

'Beware of false prophets, who come to you in sheep's
clothing but inwardly are ravenous wolves. You will
know them by their fruits. Are grapes gathered from
thorns, or figs from thistles? In the same way, every

good tree bears good fruit, but the bad tree bears bad fruit. A good tree cannot bear bad fruit, nor can a bad tree bear good fruit. Every tree that does not bear good fruit is cut down and thrown into the fire. Thus you will know them by their fruits.

'Not everyone who says to me, "Lord, Lord," will enter the kingdom of heaven, but only the one who does the will of my Father in heaven. On that day many will say to me, "Lord, Lord, did we not prophesy in your name, and cast out demons in your name, and do many deeds of power in your name?" Then I will declare to them, "I never knew you; go away from me, you evildoers."' (*Matthew 7:12–23*)

Fifteenth Station: Listen

'Everyone then who hears these words of mine and acts on them will be like a wise man who built his house on rock. The rain fell, the floods came, and the winds blew and beat on that house, but it did not fall, because it had been founded on rock. And everyone who hears these words of mine and does not act on them will be like a foolish man who built his house on sand. The rain fell, and the floods came, and the winds blew and beat against that house, and it fell – and great was its fall!

'Now when Jesus had finished saying these things, the crowds were astounded at his teaching, for he taught them as one having authority, and not as their scribes.' (*Matthew 7:24–9*)

Stations of Reality

These are guided meditations rather than stations, to be strictly honest, but we can use them in the same way, as a technique to break up a journey, or divide up the time in a day. They can be done one at a time, when we stop moving and walking. We can read them while we sit, and then perhaps carry them in our minds, walking as we go, until the next time we stop. We can also use them as a one-off meditation, spending more time exploring a single topic. There are too many to use them all in one go, so select what you need from them. Perhaps only one, or no more than three or four would be enough for one day. They should give you a new, productive direction for thought, and a new angle on the reality we inhabit and our experience of it. Read them through slowly, perhaps even aloud (try not to alarm innocent bystanders!) and let them spark off thoughts and ideas within you; let them be fuel for insight. Reality is where God is, and these are ways of exploring that place, ways of being in it with God. Indeed, the subjects of most of these meditations we can take as *signs* of God, pointing towards him, indications of presence.

The meditations are in two forms. One is experiential, where we are invited to just hear, just see, just feel, just smell or taste without discussion and thought in so far as possible, but being aware of the reality of our feelings and experience in the moment. The other form is more discursive, inviting thought and mental conversation, exploring something with our minds, but always referring to and being aware of our present experience and the feelings and sensations which arise

231

in us. Both these styles are good ways of learning, and allowing change in ourselves. They are ways of making us more aware of our surroundings and of ourselves within them. Our place in reality.

All meditation and prayer is good for us, but the temptation is to keep it for only when we feel like it, or to keep it safely packed away into formal periods; church on Sunday, for example. What is important is to bring the insights, the glimpses of reality, into our whole lives, so that we are constantly, consciously in God's presence. That's a high ideal, but it is one shared by more than Christianity. Being awake and aware and alert; seeing the truth, and not just listening to the drivel of our own minds. It's no good to go somewhere and have an experience; we must bring that experience back with us and allow it to change us and become part of us.

Gratitude

A common thread that you might like to bring to all the meditations here, which works through all of them, even the final death meditation, is the sense of gratitude. It even works well as a stand alone meditation in its own right. Think of when you were grateful for something someone did for you, or gave you. How did that feel? Where was it within your body, what was the sensation like? Spend a few moments recollecting it, experiencing it. It is a good feeling. Bring that to mind at some stage in each of these meditations; it's probably a good way to end each one of them. Take time in awareness of the gratitude within you as a wordless prayer; for the ability to sense and experience the reality around you, but also for being part of it, part of its process and movement, not separate from it, but a product of it, an end and a beginning, a cause and an effect, coming from it and going back into it; held in attention and considerate care by God, in God.

Air

We don't usually notice air, unless there's a gale blowing. Or unless we really need it – if we fall into water, for instance. Talk sometime to someone with asthma or emphysema to find out what it's like not to be able to breathe properly. The panic, the effort, the sheer hard work just to get a breath. We can do without food for weeks, a few days without water. Without air, we have two or three minutes. It is an integral, immediate part of our living process. To pay attention to the breath is to pay attention to life itself. In Hebrew, the word *ruach* means breath, wind, mind, Spirit. The Lord breathes life into humanity in Genesis, Christ breathes the Holy Spirit into the disciples (John 20). Breath and spirit and life are seen as signs for the same thing.

You can see how at the end of each complete inhalation and exhalation, at the end of each complete breath, we die in a sense. A few times each minute, we go through a small death; then we breathe in again. Someone said that the distance between life and death is only one breath. We are always that close. Our death is only a breath away. Air is that important to us.

Our breathing is mostly automatic. Breathing meditation is nothing more then than sitting, quiet and still, and becoming aware of this movement of the life-giving air out and in, over and over, as your body breathes you into being, all on its own.

We only borrow this air. It is only with us for a short while. It is another common tie with all other living beings, this mouthful of air, this breathing, this urgent need, this life.

Meditation

Be aware for a moment of the movement of the air on your skin as you walk or sit. Keep your awareness on the cool caress of the breeze, produced by your passing, or the wind blowing on you. Feel it on your hair, your eyes. Then be aware of the sensation of the air going in and going out, in your nose, your throat, your chest rising and falling. Be aware of it in your body, in your blood, in every cell of your being, bringing life and existence and consciousness. Be aware of it blowing the fires of your metabolism, producing heat, reddening your skin. Be aware of the desperate need for air you have as you walk uphill, the merciless hunger for it your body has, over which you have little control. Not like thirst, or hunger, this is immediate, this is now, this is living on the very edge of existence, the place where we are all the time, but never think of, with always only one breath between your life and your death. Cold in, warm out, down into the intimate depths of your body, and then out again, over and over and over until your last breath. This is your life, passing in and out of your nose and lips, the unseen life-giving Spirit, the Spark firing off our two-stroke heart, flowing to all of our living cells.

Walking Meditation

As you walk, pay attention to your breathing. Feel whether it is hard or soft, fast or slow. Is the air warm or cold in your throat, your nose? Be with the sensations for a while. Don't judge or qualify them, just watch, just feel.

Are you out of breath? If you are, try to hold one breath and experience the deep, urgent, nearly violent need for air your body has, to exist, to keep on living.

Just walk, counting the steps you take with each breath. So many in, so many out. Every step, every breath, a new moment, a gift of life. Stay with that immediate experience of life for as long as you can.

Fire

From fire our world, our universe came. From solar fusion and in the magma beneath us on which continental plates float and bang together to make mountains. Fire is the sign of activity, of motion, of change, of things happening. The opposite is found only in the long, cold reaches of space outside the universe, beyond the borders our minds can travel to. Away from sound and sight and light and heat. Away from nebula, galaxy, solar system and home, where there is nothing to change, nothing to be changed, in the eternal cold.

Fire is the mark of change, reaction and growth; it produces light, heat and life, dust and ashes. It is the sign of moving from one state to another. The absence of fire is not death, but sameness, immutability. Total, absolute cold, where no molecules vibrate, no energy exists. Metamorphosis and impermanence are the marks of life and of existence. All things change, and when they change, there is fire. Heat.

The star that pumps heat into our planet, into us, ensures that life and change can occur. The fire that powers the photosynthesis of plants, that heats the air and oceans, is a part of what we are. The heat of our skins, our breath, is sunlight passing through the conduit of life – from the sun, to plants and animals and then to us through our food.

Change also means that nothing can ever stay the same, everything is, must be, in constant flux; order from chaos, structure ground down by entropy. Growth and ageing are the two sides of the mountain of our lives. To live is to be changed.

Meditation

Touch something living. Someone's shoulder or face or arm – or your own! A dog, a horse. Or failing all that, turn your face to the sun, if it's shining. We give out heat, but other living things, plants, reptiles, use the heat of the world around them to live, they borrow it from the sun. Become aware of the heat in your own body, or in another's body. This is sunlight caught and transmuted through food to keep you alive and functioning. The heat is a sign of change and life. You are the total effect of many processes within you: liver, heart, brain, digestion, kidneys, immune system, all working together to produce you. You are the total of many things coming together in one place, at one time. Evolution, history, chance, design, intention, all trickle down through millennia and here you are. The fire in your body comes from the sun, the plants, the animals, the cells in your body, all channelled to continue your existence. We are change walking around on two legs.

If it's a cold day, feel your hand, your nose, your toes (or someone else's!). Become aware of the cold in them, realise it's the absence of life-giving heat, and that the process of cooling is one that leads to frostbite – the death of living cells. Or to exposure and the total death of your organism. Heat, borrowed sunlight, is essential to our life and survival. Look deeply and understand how heat and cold mean life and death.

Tongues of flame were a mark of the Holy Spirit in the story of Pentecost in the Acts of the Apostles: 'And suddenly from heaven there came a sound like the rush of a violent wind, and it filled the entire house where they were sitting. Divided tongues, as of fire, appeared among them, and a tongue rested on each of them. All of them were filled with the Holy Spirit' (Acts 2). This is a mark of new life, of the presence of the Spirit of God, a mark of change and growth.

Walking Meditation

Be aware of the fire within and around you. Perhaps in the sun shining on you, or in an opposite sense, perhaps the wind and rain cooling you. Perhaps the heat you are generating within yourself from walking uphill, your muscles working, blood sloshing around your system, chemistry happening to power your movement, food digested and channelled into life. All of the processes giving out heat. What is the sensation? Dwell with it as you walk along, allow your attention to stay with it. It is the sign of your living organism. It is the sign of change, both growth and decay. Be aware of the living processes within you, within the plants and animals and other people around you.

Water

Water comes as steam, ice and snow, mist and fog, fine rain, and droplets slapping you as they fall heavily out of the sky. Then the trickles and splashes of young streams, fast-flowing rivers, surging sea. Or as living, walking beings, like us.

Water is in constant recycling free fall and flow, pushed and pulled by wind and current and lunar gravity. Castles and mountains and whole countries of it float and hang in the air far above us, then when the point of the Reek impales the belly of the cloud, the breeze makes the raggedy, cloudy entrails stream from the mountain top, far into the bay.

This element is what runs in our veins, keeps the membrane of each cell taut, is seventy per cent of the life in us, the ingredient that is the medium of our moving and being and breathing. The steam of our breath, the tears of our eyes, the spit of our mouths. Urine and mucus, semen and sweat, blood and bile, the universal solvent on which, through which, in which, life exists and breeds and feeds and dies and disperses. All living things are addicted to this stuff like no other drug in the world, from birth we float in it, roll in it, drink it, inhale it. We are water, upright, walking.

This is the lifeblood of our baptism, the soul of our tears, the spirit of our breath. This is what makes all life be possible. This water within us has run already through all the living beings that have ever been, can ever be. This water is holy, blessed, consecrated by every being that has ever taken it in, lived by it, and passed it on. Molecules of the water that rolled off Christ's head at his baptism, the sweat that dripped off his face in the Garden, are the same ones that baptised us, slaked our thirst, rained on us. The water that will be used to wash us on our deathbeds is the same water from which we were given birth.

Meditation

Touch water. Sweat or spit, or the dew on the grass, a puddle. Or hold your hand to catch the rain. All the same. The same water that runs through your veins, down your face, the tears of your eyes. There is no other water. The water of baptism, the water of life, the water of plastic bottles, the water of blood, of rain. The water from Christ's side. Touch this water, be with it, feel it and see the light on it, the reflection in it. Dirty or clean, salty or fresh; through the sea, through the air, through the clouds, through the rain, through the stream, the river, the groundwater, the bog, the plant, through your body, through the bird, the animal, the factory. There is no other water, there is only this. Living water.

Walking Meditation

Be aware of the water around you. In the ground, in the air, in your breath. See the other people, animals, birds, growing things, as walking water, growing water, living water, bags of water walking around, flying, living. Feel the liquid element in your body, in all aspects of your body, taking shape, standing, moving. The weight and swing and flow. The sweat on your skin; saliva in your mouth; tears in your eyes, steam in your breath. The weight of your body is mostly water. Or (if you're reading this in Ireland!) pay full attention to the rain as it falls; the sensation on your skin, the noise it makes, how it wets things, what it looks like in the air, the smell of it. Or notice the drying effect of breathing hard through your mouth as you ascend the mountain. Feel what thirst is like, when the notion of taking a drink of water comes to you. Hesitate before you drink. What does this need, this desire for water feel like? Where is it in your body? How does it manifest itself?

A final suggestion: use the 'white noise' of a stream as a meditation. Just listen to the water. Ignore thoughts or thinking if it comes up, as best you can. Just concentrate on the sound the water makes as it flows. Sit or stand, and become enrapt in one of the most basic, ancient and important sounds ever heard in our world.

Stone

Stone seems very different from us, alien. It is hard and cold, sharp or rounded. Rough or smooth. Not soft, not warm, not growing, not sentient. Stones are objects to be used, built with, piled up, thrown, tripped over; for walls and weapons, divisions and separations. Stone walls create meanings, a building, a house, a temple, a home, a barn, a factory, a field. Stone boundaries define and control the landscape. They engrave human ideas on to it. Stone walls are an attempt to force permanency.

Stone seems like time frozen, but that's just the perception of ephemeral creatures like us. Stone moves and flows, dissolves and grows at its own pace, very far removed from ours. Stone is solid, visible minerals and nutrients, metals and chemicals. The skeleton of the world. Stone is the unimaginable stuff of stars, the remnants of deserts or seas, hot planet spewings from the inner core.

But stone is also our skeleton, our teeth; dissolved in water it is our blood, our tears. We are not separate or different. It is a part of us, part of life. Within the stones, the stop-frame de-animation of fossils, dinosaurs, diatom shells is proof of it. We are our ancestors recycled, we are a product, a step in the process of life. The stone we see around us is a step in a slower process of erosion and sediment, pressure, cold and immense heat. Existence, but at another speed.

Meditation
A. Pick up a piece of stone. Examine it. Take your time. Look at the colours, the shine, the glitter, the texture, the weight. Look at the shape of it. Is it sharp edged, a fragment off a larger

rock, or rounded, a stone on its own? What made it this way? Wind? Water? Fire? Frost splitting it; glaciers rubbing it; streams, the sea rolling it? Taste it, perhaps. Feel it on your tongue like a young child would. Be with it for a while. It is a chunk of reality, just like yourself.

What are its origins? It is born from fire? Squeezed, extruded from the belly of the earth, hardening, cracking, glowing once with the light of stars, and then dimming to the hard, cold normality we can pick up and handle.

Or is it the child of water, did it form beneath a great sea, pressed, frozen now into immovability, solidity? Did desert winds once mix its grains together before it hardened to stone? Was it once wet mud? What creatures lived and died in it, left their bones in it, flowered and withered in it? What creatures compose it? If it is limestone, it is entirely the fossil of life, the stony mummy of countless living animals. A snapshot in death, preserved for millions of years

How did it get here? Remember just for a moment the path it has travelled to be where you are, and how that connects with your path just here and now. This place, this time, this weather, this day and year, this juncture in your life. A snapshot of reality.

B. Pick up a stone, a rock, sand. Hold it and feel it and be with it as before. Feel the stone, the minerals. The hardness, the texture, the difference between the softness of skin, of living tissue and the sharpness, the rough and smooth of stone. Bring into your mind the crystals, the chemicals, the molecules which go to make it up, which go to make you up. The solidity of your skeleton, the hardness of your teeth, the silica of your nails and hair is all one with sand and rock and mud and chalk. It is part of us, and we of it. It is the ingredient, together with water, which gives us shape, that which is not air or fire or water, which lets us come together, be solid, stand, move, differentiate ourselves. The bones of the earth are in our bones, this gritty dust and ashes left by burning stars is a major ingredient in us. We are one with this place, a product of it.

Walking Meditation
Become aware of your bony skeleton, the rigidity within yourself which allows you to move, to stand, to be erect. Become aware of the joints, the mechanism which lets you walk, bend, stretch. Become aware of the muscles working against and with the bony levers of your body, arms and legs, back and belly, and your ribs and chest and diaphragm letting you breathe; your jaw, your teeth. Look at other people or animals nearby, see the skeleton within them, allowing their animation, their movement, supporting their structure. Perceive them as walking skeletons.

As you move along, concentrate on each bone, or set of bones in your body: the parts of your head, face, and jaw, shoulders, arms and hands, shoulder blades, ribs, spine, pelvis and femurs, lower legs and feet. Or move your consciousness from one joint to another, jaws, neck, shoulders, elbows and so on. Take a short time with each one, and become aware of your skeleton that way.

Hear the crunch of small stones and rocks beneath your feet as you go along. Feel the crucial solidity of rock as you walk over it, ungiving, unmoving. Feel the textures against the soles of your footwear, or on your bare feet. This stone, this rock is part of you; its nature is common to you and to itself. It is part of what we are, and we are part of it, but conscious, walking around, thinking and talking and reproducing.

Soil

The soil, the stuff that plants grow in, that covers the rocks and bones of the Earth, is the medium for all growing, living things to exist on or in. All those on dry land, anyway. Soil is made up of sand and grit and minerals and water and decayed animal and vegetable life, and in and through and past that is a hiving, thriving, living mass of microbes and insects and bacteria and fungi and invertebrates.

It's not just soil. Not just dirt, or black or brown stuff. It's as important to us as our own flesh and blood, or should be. Nothing grows, nothing lives, nothing moves on the dry land of this planet that hasn't some intimate, crucial connexion with this stuff. You don't have to dig down very far in most places to discover that it's only a thin layer on the top of the world's crust. Perhaps only a few inches, or in lucky places a few feet deep. Below it is subsoil, comparatively sterile. But the black humus, the rich soil of the world is heaving and teeming with life and promise and potential. This soil has been laid down, millennium after millennium. It is made up of the dust and bones and leaves and twigs, skin and hair of our ancestors – the countless millions of animals and insects, plants and people, big, small and microscopic, who came before us. The heritage of our living companions on the planet. Soil is an integral part of the living biosphere. It is very, very precious. It is not just a sterile medium for plants to grow in, it is nearly alive in its own right, a living skin, an animated carpet.

Meditation
Take up a pinch of soil from the ground. On the Reek, on an Irish mountain, it may be dark, wet, boggy stuff, and even

with the naked eye, you can see it is not just a simple homogenous substance. It has bits in it; bits of dead plants, the wing case of a beetle, perhaps, grains of sand, pieces of twig and heather and moss. There's every chance that a small pinch, the burden of a thumb and two fingers, will contain millions and millions of tiny lives. Creatures striving and eating and breeding and dying. Spores of fungi, seeds waiting to hatch the new life within them. This is what we are made of. This is what we come from. This is where we go after we are alive. This is the manna that gives us bread and air, that feeds the animals we eat and live with. This has the bones of your predecessors in it, their sloughed off skin cells. The soil you hold in your hand is part of you, keeps you in life, fills your lungs with air. It is a precious gift, an inheritance without price. Treasure it for a moment, before returning it to the ground.

Walking Meditation
Feel the soil under your feet, the different texture it has from the rock, or a hard path. It is softer, yielding. It interacts with our weight. Plants and trees can dig down deep into it, feed on it. How many animalcules, bacteria, living teeming things live in it, go to make it up? This is not an inert substance, it is nearly a complex organism in its own right. Let your feet caress it, care for it as you walk along. Become aware of growing things in it. Not just grass, not just leaves, but lives. Watch where your feet go, be aware for a while of how one footstep of yours can affect the life of a complex growing thing, injuring, destroying. Be aware of the life beneath your feet, life intimately connected with your own, the heritage bequeathed you by your ancestors, plant, animal, fungus, microbe, and human.

Light

We don't usually see light. Light is what we see by, see in, see with. We only see or notice it when there isn't enough or there's too much and our eyes can't function. In between we just see. Light is neither wave nor particle solely, it moves at speeds where our minds can't go and there are too many zeros to understand. It is beyond our ken in any human sense. Maths and physics might go some way to grasping it, but not an unadorned human.

Light is not just about seeing. Light is half of the life the sun gives us. The heat of the sun, the fire we can feel on our skin is part of the story. The other part is the light that fires off the chemistry in the bottom storey of the pyramid of life, in algae and plants, the secret ingredient that allows our human boat to float at the top on the layers and layers of life beneath us. This is the engine room of the world, making the sugars and oxygen to give life and to empower everything else. Light is something that the world, our planet, is not self-sufficient in. Were the light to suddenly stop, the sun be switched off, almost all life would quite rapidly grind to a halt, the power source removed, the carpet of chlorophyll pulled from beneath us. Light is a part of us, built into us, at a level so basic, so fundamental that we are unaware of it. It is one of the ingredients of being alive. Our ancestors' deification of the sun in most cultures was reasonable enough. It rules day and night, seasons, food and comfort and finally and totally, survival. Lugh, the Celtic god whose birth feast (Lughnasa) falls at the time of Reek Sunday, is thought to have been a sun god.

Light is a frequent symbol in the Bible. It is the first thing to be created in Genesis, and in the Gospel of John, Christ styles himself as the 'light of the world'. It is a symbol of goodness, hope and of clear perception and understanding.

Meditation

Our eyes are the organs we have to detect light, to differentiate the wavelengths, the colours it comes in. What our minds do with the details of that, the final analysis the brain makes of the information received through that light, we call seeing. Try to become aware of seeing, aware of what your mind is doing with the light hitting your eyes. Learning to draw is one way of doing that. Putting down on paper the lines, the shading, the perspective your eyes are detecting, and your mind interpreting. Try to draw what you see, however inexpertly, and remain aware of the process of seeing.

As you eat some food, do it mindfully. Take every piece of food before you put it in your mouth, and spend time with it, remember where it came from, what went into its growth, its being in your hand, here, now, today, and who and what had a part in getting it to you. The farmer, the soil, the air and water, the light and heat, the producer and shopkeeper. Whoever prepared it for you to eat. Or trace the lines the energy, the sunlight has followed to give you continued existence and life itself. Whatever food we eat is based on the life and death of other organisms, and the root of all the life on the planet, in one way or another, is the light of the sun.

When you put the food in your mouth, take time to experience the shape and feel of it before you bite into it. Take time to fully experience the taste, the separate parts of the flavour in different parts of your mouth. Chew it slowly, taking your time with it, and remaining aware of what you're doing. Then after you swallow, experience the aftertaste, the fading sensations. This is sunlight you're eating, whatever it is. This is life. Take a moment to be grateful.

Walking Meditation
Seeing isn't a simple thing. What comes up inside our minds when we look at something has been processed and analysed and judged before we receive the images in our consciousness. Our minds, our subconscious, our conditioning has all had a good look at the pictures before we get them.

Become aware of how you see, how there is a hidden commentary that accompanies each image in your mind. These aren't just pictures in your head, you know what these things are. You like or dislike them, or feel neutral towards them. You have names for them all. How would a gardener, a carpenter, a sculptor, a firewood producer and a dog perceive a tree? They won't see the same thing in the same way.

Watch yourself and try to apprehend how you see people as you go along. You compartmentalise them without thinking. You are interested in some, reject others, are wary of some and find others attractive, or perhaps beneath your attention entirely. Your mind has done all this for you! Be aware that what you see isn't what's there, it's what your mind thinks is there. The reality of anything we see resides within itself, not in our judgments and opinions of it.

We use 'seeing' to mean 'understanding' but there is actually a big gap between the two things! Seeing *can* be perceiving, but you must bring a conscious effort of will to achieve it, looking deeply, intently, closely. Seeing with the eyes of the heart, as they say, and always remembering that our understanding of the other will never be total.

Sound

We can use sound as an object for meditation. It's not hard, once you learn a bit of concentration. But even if you only get a few moments strung together here and there, it still works and brings benefits.

Hearing and listening are not the same thing. We hear constantly, but our minds filter out what they want, or feel they need to hear. We rarely listen to all that is going on at the same time, or simply experience the soundscape we inhabit without selection or judgement.

Sit somewhere with your eyes closed. Or stand. Compose yourself for a moment. Then listen to what's going on around you. Don't listen to any one bit of it, if you can, listen to all of it, going on at the same time. Don't be selective. Try to avoid places where there is music or human voices to be heard, as they will surely distract you. Listen to nature, or cars or city noises, the sea, the wind, water. Don't identify or name anything as one thing or another, just let the sounds come and go.

After a while, with a bit of practice, you will hear noises happen and stop, and you won't feel the need to think about them, or follow them with your mind or analyse them. They are just experiences happening in your life, your ears, your head. The sound of a stream, or the sea is perhaps easier to do this with. Don't go to sleep, don't space out, remain aware and awake. Just you and the sounds. Try, after a while, to become aware of the spaces between the sounds, the gaps. The silences, or indeed the Silence that lies behind the sound, beneath it and around it, is that which allows it to be. Enter deeply into the sense of hearing, of listening. All these sound waves, all this noise, most of which we are not aware of, is going on constantly. Our minds pick and choose amongst them. They follow a noise, or pick a thread out of the weave; this particular voice, this specific tone. But the whole thing is there always, if we choose to listen without distinction. Bearing it up, giving it a background to exist in and against, is the silence. Silence is a symbol for God.

> Elijah went to Horeb the mount of God. At that place he came to a cave, and spent the night there. Then the word of the Lord came to him, saying, 'Go out and stand on the mountain before the Lord, for the Lord is about to pass by.' Now there was a great wind, so strong that it was splitting mountains and breaking rocks in pieces before the Lord, but the Lord was not in the wind; and after the wind an earthquake, but the Lord was not in the earthquake; and after the earthquake a fire, but the Lord was not in the fire; and after the fire a sound of sheer silence. When Elijah heard it, he wrapped his face in his mantle and went out and stood at the entrance of the cave.
>
> (*1 Kings 19*)

God is not in the fire, the wind, or the earthquake, God is in the silence.

The silence is not destroyed by the sound, or wiped out, or disturbed. The silence continues, even while noise, sound is happening. The silence is always there. Listen for it sometime. It is not a bad thing, or a scary thing. Silence is potential, it is the emptiness that allows for something to happen, something to fill, something to be a noise within and beside it. Silence is the prerequisite for sound, pervades sound, defines sound, enlivens it and allows it to be distinguished, separate for a while. Silence is the abyss from which all comes, and in and by which all exists. Silence is the sound that space makes, that contains all things and allows them to exist. Silence and emptiness are the preconditions for existence. They are another face of God.

Walking Meditation

You can do sound meditation while walking, of course. Be aware of the sound of your own breath, your body, your heart, your lungs. The sound of your feet, of the wind, of water and whatever else is around you. Perhaps zero in on one particular facet of the soundscape you are in, name and identify it, then name another and another, and then finally pull back the focus so that you are aware of all the sounds, but let the naming, the identifying, the following stop, and just keep bringing your mind back again and again to the sounds. Here is the noise that life makes, that reality makes, that existence makes, happening in your ears and your mind, and you are adding to it as you go along.

Now

There are two ways to deal with 'now', this present fleeting moment which is the only one we exist in. One is to have a good think about what now is, what time is, what our experience of the world is, what past and future, and the here and now are, for example. There is a thinking meditation below this doing just that.

The other way of dealing with now is through awareness, pure awareness; just feeling this, seeing that, hearing this, without thinking about it, or talking to yourself about it. Just experiencing what's happening now, whatever comes along. That's keeping your mind focussed on *this* moment, *this* experience of now. Then the next moment, and the next. This is a kind of meditation, known as *Shikantaza*, and it takes a good bit of practice to sustain it. It is a complete contact with reality insofar as we humans can experience it. It is the truth, without our childish scrawls and doodles all over the top of it, colouring it in with our opinions and ideas and judgements.

Thinking, discursive thought, has its place and is necessary. In terms of spirituality, though, the best thing to do is to trust. To trust that God is there, that God is keeping it all – this now, this episode and thin slice of the truth – in existence, and in a loving existence. Trust in that, have faith in it, and experience your own personal serving of the truth, of reality, of now, brought to you by your senses: wind on skin, air in lungs, pulsing heart, eyes filled with rocks and grass and heather, sun or rain, bright sky or mist, ground underfoot, sweat, effort, straining muscles, working body. That is enough. There isn't any more. It is what is freely given to us, it is the experience of living, of now, that most of us miss because we are always too busy in our lives, or in our minds. To add religion and prescribed beliefs and dogmas to all of this may be to miss it all over again. Jesus didn't teach a complicated theology course, he wasn't giving us detailed myths and liturgical instructions. He was telling us how to relate to God, how to get on with other people, how to live. Thinking is good, but living is the point in the end.

Meditation

How long is the moment we call now? Is it the tiniest micro-second wide, or is it a couple of seconds? Think about what now means, what it contains. What is going on within it? The now of our experience is restricted to the small circle of what we can hear and see and feel and smell and think. This now contains all that is, and all that potentially will be. It's where God is. Because God contains all, and causes all to exist. But notice that once we bring all that to mind we've started imagining and talking to ourselves again. We're not just experiencing now, we're thinking about it, and judging it and enjoying it or wishing it could be a different kind of experience.

Look around you, realise what all around you means, where it comes from, what it signifies, what it points to. How it got to be with you today, what its travels were through time, what its origins where. Do that for a number of living or inanimate objects around you. Think of what made them come together, the raw materials of them, how they evolved and changed down the generations, or how they were made, by whom, who first thought of them. Then think back where the raw materials come from, the origins of the world, evolution, stars, celestial dust clouds coalescing, the big bang, creation itself. Before that again, where both science and religion agree that there was no time, no space. No now, and no here.

Realise then that this is still going on. This is a process, not finished, never arrived at. You yourself, this place, these things around you are not the end point, this is one of many, many moments. Creation isn't something that happened once upon a time. In our human imaginations sometimes it's as if the earthly stage we strut about on only reaches back for the few thousand years of our recorded history, and we're only in the second act of a three act play, the present sandwiched between an imagined and remembered past, and an imagined future. But we have found out that our imaginations are more limited than we think. We only have ten fingers to count on, but the universe counts on more digits than we can contemplate. The numbers soar and swoop, not just in the outer astronomical reaches of the cosmos, and not only in the teeming life at the microscopic level of cell and bacteria and virus, but within matter itself, beneath the skin of atomic nuclei, down into a quantum universe and other dimensions.

We too are process, not the finished article, not an end product. We are not the newborn child still, any more than we are the witless teenager, or the bright-eyed young adult, or middle aged, or old. These are all stages we pass through; no one state defines us. Death is another stage of process, we believe. One we cannot see beyond, but process is a better way of thinking about it than just finality, or eternity without change. God may be more in the change than in the eternal changelessness we ascribe to him anyway.

At the same time, process is only a theory, another idea; more words and opinions. The only proof we have, the only certainty, is this single moment. This slice of feeling and experience coming through our senses. Then the next one. Even as one comes along, the last has ceased to exist and the next is only a hope, another opinion. Concept becomes reality only for an instant, to then become memory. That's what we call process. The process of now is what our existence consists of. As for God, now is where we can read the signs of his presence, and the only place we are in his presence.

Plants

Weeds, trees, bushes, herbs, plants, mosses, grass, heather. Some of them you can eat, most of them you can't. Some have nice flowers. Most humans have little time for any growing plant which isn't beautiful, useful or edible. But these are the lungs of the world, these are the solar cells which turn sunlight into food, this is the way the whole living system of the world powers itself. Light is taken into leaves and made into food. The plant lives; the animals live; the people live. The very grass and plants beneath our feet that we tune out, that we walk on, every living fibre of them is giving us life, giving life to life. They are the source of our oxygen, our spirit/breath, they are the source of our food, in themselves or as condiment and flavour. They are medicine for our bodies, they are beauty for our eyes and minds.

They are also an 'alien life form' without perceptible movement, living, growing, propagating and dying in a very different way from ours. Plants perceive reality differently too. Without eyes or ears but tuned to light, to water, to minerals, they shoulder living space for themselves, vanquish enemies, pests and parasites. They breed through wind and insect-borne pollen, scattering their seeds, pushing upwards into the light. Always the light. They turn to the sun with green leaves spread to receive the gift of light, of life.

Meditation
Feel some grass growing near you. Let your hands play with it, and it play with your hands, stroke it, feel it, experience it. Smell it. Look at it as if for the first time. You have just been let out of prison, or just born, and this is the first grass you've

seen ever! Be with it, drink in all the details of it. Then pick a stalk of it. Have a good look at it, the way it is made, the distinct textures of it, shiny bits, rough bits, hard and soft and thin and thick. Then perhaps chew a bit of it, taste it with your eyes closed, the feel of it on your tongue and mouth, the distinct parts of the flavours within the taste: sweet/bitter/sour. The aftertaste of it, the fibres, the crunchy bits. This is the powerhouse of our planet, turning sun into food. Perhaps not food for us directly, but for sheep and cattle and other animals all over the globe. This and other plants, this very greenness is the light of the sun made solid, made flesh, if you like. Waves of energy made into life.

Walking Meditation
Watch where you're walking and what you're walking on. If it's green, it's alive, just like you. Think about that.

Animal

If you can find a handy animal or insect or fish, something living, with legs or wings or fins, something animated, well and good. Take a good look at it, study it, see it, feel it, smell it, listen to it, be with it, try to feel and experience what it must/might be feeling. Touch it if you can. (But since you yourself are a specimen, you yourself might have to do, depending on where you are!)

Animals are inert matter bundled together in such a way that they are alive, animated. This mixture of minerals and water is walking around the place! Think about what alive means for a moment: What is it? What is that spark, that animation that makes the difference? Beware of giving yourself glib, easy answers you maybe got somewhere else on your travels – the breath of God, or just a chance alignment of molecules. Think about it, not with words and sentences but with feelings and pictures and intuition. Try to get a grasp of this slippery concept of Life.

Whatever organism you are contemplating is very like you. Very close to you. Through evolution all living things are related, but with most of them the relation is so distant that we might feel little connection. There is a closer tie. To be alive at all is to share the close, tight, personal and immediate need and drive tied to all life. That is to avoid pain and suffering, and to seek happiness, whether that happiness lies in food or sex, or heat or light, or moisture or dryness or darkness. Whatever the best situation may be on the one hand, contrasted with the worst on the other. Organisms know and choose and strive all in the same way. From the simplest single-celled organisms, through invertebrates and up into the more complex animals (and even in plants), this drive is common to all of us. It is the basis of life. We wish to be happy, and we wish to avoid suffering. Look at whatever animal you have to hand and understand that. Realise the connection, the closeness, the depth at which you can understand the Other. We are not different, we are very much the same, whether we have two or four or six or eight legs, fins, wings, pseudopods or cilia. Good and bad are realities for all of us. All the living beings striving on this planet. One major difference is that as humans we can know this, we can imagine it, inhabit it, intuit it, and respond to it, thus we can learn compassion for the life around us; pity and sympathy and love and care. Or we can ignore the fact, and pretend ignorance of the feeling and experience of the rest of living reality. Religious faith encourages us towards that fellow feeling, that compassion, that understanding of the other at a basic level, so that we might be moved to help, to assist, or at the very least to refrain from harm or hurt.

Meditation
As a meditation, you might like to try the loving-kindness meditation in Chapter Seven. You can do this sitting or walking along, for whichever living beings you come across, including yourself.

Death

All this talk of life implies, needs, death as part of it. Life and death are closer than two sides of a coin, they are not separate things, they are part of the same thing.

Death is important. It is the one inevitable, certain and definite fact about your life and all lives. There will be an end to this for each of us. Old age, illness, decrepitude, seeing things and people we love pass away will happen to most of us. Some of us will die so soon, we may not even see our own growing old, our running down, fading. Or so suddenly we may not see death coming. But death is certain for all. So thinking about it, realising it, making it a facet of living, and not in a morbid way, is a good thing, a wise thing, a helpful thing. Death is not the enemy; there are worse things out there than dying. Death brings separation and sadness, but can also bring the peace and healing that are the end of pain and suffering. Death is a part of life, not just the end of it, or the opposite to it.

It pays to sit and think about it. To visualise it, to see what would happen if *I* died, *I* was no longer here, was over, gone, finished in the world. There is a meditation below to guide us in seeing how the ripples of the surface of the world will gently close over the space we leave after us.

It pays to realise the value, the importance of our life, this existence, this moment. Sometimes the only thing that will wake us up enough is the realisation of our deaths, putting our death beside our life, so that we clearly see the contrast: the bright, essential, priceless spark on the one hand, and the simple, dark, total, absence on the other.

We can use our deaths to fulfil our lives. Living with the reality and inevitability of our deaths constantly beside us, as a true measure and yardstick of the values and experiences we come across in life. Place anything beside your death as a comparison and see the truth of it, the inherent meaning and value of it, without fantasy or fooling ourselves. See those we love acquire their true stature and importance, see money and fame and the other nonsense we blind ourselves with, shrink to their true proportions, show their true skin and features. Use your death to see your life, your reality as it truly is, in its true perspective.

This is a way of seeing how God sees. Seeing reality without our overlying perceptions, preferences and opinions. This is one way to see truth. Or rather Truth. Truth is where God is, what God sees, what God is. We can get glimpses of it, hints of it. It is the kingdom Jesus spoke of where important things are truly important and we can tell the difference. Where the poor, the mourners, and the persecuted are blessed.

The meditation below is not meant to make you sad or emotional, though that might happen if you get deeply involved in it. It's intended to help you see your life from another standpoint. It's meant to give a perspective that might not occur to you very often. Try to look, hard though it might be, cooly, detachedly, without judging or condemning. Just watch.

Meditation
Think for a moment of your own, actual death. In a bed, sick at home or in hospital, when you're not much older than you are now. Perhaps just next week. Think of who will miss you when the funeral is over, the last sod thrown on the grave, the last mourner gone home. Who will go to their beds this night with a sore, aching heart? Your immediate, close family, fair enough, but who else? Who else have you touched in your life who will remember you? Spend a short time with this.

Now you're no longer there, what about your belongings? The things you owned? A house, perhaps, a car, books, a computer, pets, land, music, photographs, clothes and shoes. A watch, a phone. All the objects you used in the kitchen, around the house, the garden. Who has them now? Did you really ever own them? Or the money. The numbers in a bank statement, or on a payslip that you worked for? Where is that now? Where was it ever, other than on paper, in a computer?

What about your work, your job? Who would take your place? Who will be at your desk, your place in production, on the work floor, at the counter; who will teach your class, drive your vehicle, make the decisions? How long will it be before the ripples of your absence fade? In what way will you be remembered there, in six months, in a year, five years? Take a moment and think about that.

In your own locality, your town or city or area, who knew you had died? What lives did yours nudge up against? Who were you friendly with, close to? Did you have 'enemies', people who didn't like you, who had a grudge against you? Will they remember you? Or will you slip totally out of their minds once you're gone? Take another moment to deal with this.

How do you think people will picture you in five years time, if your name comes up in conversation? What will stand out? What will last? What will no longer be important or remembered? What will drop off? Your children, if you have any, will remember you, but what will they remember? Will your grandchildren even know your name? Will they know anything about you?

Look back at the fragments of your now broken life, one after another. Which bits were truly important? What did you give your attention to? What should you have paid more heed to? Who were the *really* important people? Who did you ignore that needed your attention? Is there anyone you'd fallen out with in a way that really shouldn't have happened? What do you regret doing? Or not doing? What were the blessings? What was good? What should you have done more – or less! – of when you had the chance?

How will it be in thirty, forty, fifty years time when even the broken fragments will have dissolved? Who will remember? What will have happened to all the worries, the anxieties, the fears? The preferences and dislikes? Will there be anything more than a name on a stone left? Some dust in a grave, or ashes long since scattered? What will it have meant?

When you have spent some time in contemplation of your absence, stand up, take a moment to come back to wherever you are, and remember your real presence. You are here, now, alive, in this wonderful moment, aware and conscious. You still have time – even if only to next week! Some things can be done another way if that is what is required. Some things may already be past change and may only be endured. But what happens in the future depends on how we think now. Who we are for other people depends on what we say and do and how we treat them. We have no control over how we are remembered other than how we are in ourselves in our lifetimes. The bad may or may not be recalled, but the good will bring a smile with the memory. Forgiveness is available now. Change is possible now. How we see and think is what influences how we behave now, where we end up, and what it will mean when we get there.

Don't be too harsh on yourself, or use this as an opportunity to beat yourself up. Have mercy on yourself, as God has mercy on you. Have compassion and love for yourself, even for what you might see as the bad bits, and learn from what you see, so that you can begin to move off in a new direction, if needs be.

Booklist

A few books that you may find helpful or interesting.

Croagh Patrick:

Morahan, Leo, *Croagh Patrick, Co. Mayo: Archaeology, Landscape and People* (Croagh Patrick Archaeological Committee, Westport), 2001.

Hughes, Harry (ed.), *Croagh Patrick: Ireland's Holy Mountain* (Croagh Patrick Archaeological Committee, Westport), 2005.

Hughes, Harry, *Croagh Patrick: A Place of Pilgrimage, a Place of Beauty* (O'Brien Press, Dublin), 2010.

Fahey, Frank, *Tóchar Phádraig: A Pilgrim's Progress* (Ballintubber Abbey Publications), 1989.

Meditation and Prayer:

Freeman, Laurence, *Jesus the Teacher Within* (Continuum), 2000.

—*First Sight: The Experience of Faith* (Continuum), 2011.

—*The Selfless Self* (Canterbury Press), 2009.

Main, John, OSB, *The Inner Christ* (Darton, Longman and Todd), 1987. [Christian meditation.]

The Dalai Lama, *The Good Heart* (World Community for Christian Meditation, Rider Press), 1996. [A reading of the gospels from a Buddhist perspective.]

Keating, Thomas, *Foundations for Centering Prayer and The Christian Contemplative Life* (Continuum), 2002.

Meadow, Mary Jo, *Gentling the Heart* (Crossroad), 1994.

—*Purifying the Heart* (Crossroad), 1994

—*Christian Insight Meditation: Following in the Footsteps of John of the Cross* (Wisdom), 2007.

Cowan, John, *Taking Jesus Seriously: Buddhist Meditation for Christians* (Liturgical Press), 2004.

Salzburg, Sharon, *LovingKindness: The Revolutionary Art of Happiness* (Shambala), 1997.

Olga Savin (Trans.), *The Way of a Pilgrim* (Shambala), 2001. [The Jesus Prayer.]

Palmer, Sherrard & Ware (eds), *The Philokalia*, vols 1–4 (Faber and Faber), 1979.

Waddell, Helen, *The Desert Fathers* (Constable), 1936.

Ward, Benedicta, SLG, *The Sayings of the Desert Fathers* (Cistercian Publications), 1995.

Williams, Rowan, *Silence and Honey Cakes: The Wisdom of the Desert* (Medio Media), 2003.

De Mello, Anthony, SJ, *Awareness* (Zondervan), 1990.

—*Sadhana: A Way to God* (Doubleday), 1984.

Anon., *The Cloud of Unknowing* (Penguin Classics), 1961.

Kabat-Zinn, Jon, *Wherever You Go, There You Are* (Hyperion), 1994.

—*Full Catastrophe Living* (Delta), 1990. [This is more about the medical side of mindfulness meditation, but may be of interest.]

Kornfield, Jack, *A Path with Heart: A Guide Through the Perils and Promises of Spiritual Life* (Rider), 1994. [This is a Buddhist book, but much of it is relevant to Christian spirituality as well.]

Thich Nhat Hanh and Dr Lilian Cheung, *Savor: Mindful Eating, Mindful Life* (Harper One), 2010.
Brother Lawrence, *Practice of the Presence of God*,
 [Text available online at:
 http://www.ccel.org/ccel/lawrence/practice]
Merton, Thomas, *New Seeds of Contemplation New Directions* (New Directions), 1972.
—*The Seven Storey Mountain* (Mariner Books), 1999.

It's worth having a look at books by Teresa of Avila, St John of the Cross, Meister Eckhart, and Cassian, to just name a few, if you wish to explore the older mystical and meditative tradition in Christianity.

History:
De Paor, Liam, *Saint Patrick's World* (Four Courts Press), 1993.
Sumption, Johnathan, *Pilgrimage* (Faber and Faber), 1975.
MacNeill, Máire, *The Festival of Lughnasa* (Comhairle Bhéaloideas Éireann), 2008.

Liturgy and Prayerbooks:
Common Worship: Times and Seasons (Church House Publishing), 2006.
Church of Ireland Book of Common Prayer (Columba Press), 2004.

Below are some Daily Office books. They vary in approach and in complexity. The School of Prayer is a good introduction to the Roman Office, but all of them take a bit of getting used to at the start. It may pay to change every few months or every year or so to keep your prayer and interest fresh.

Raine, Andy, *Celtic Daily Prayer* (Harper Collins), 2000.
Brook, John, *The School of Prayer: An Introduction to the Divine Office for All Christians* (Liturgical Press), 1992. [Basic instructions on how to read the Office.]

The Divine Office, *The Liturgy of the Hours according to the Roman Rite* (Talbot), 1974. [This is available in 3 volumes, with 7 services a day, or in one volume with just Morning and Evening prayer for example.]
—*Celebrating Common Prayer: A Version of The Daily Office SSF* (Mowbray), 1992.
—*Celebrating Daily Prayer* (Continuum), 2005.
Shane Claiborne, Jonathan Wilson-Hartgrove, Enuma Okoro: *Common Prayer: A Liturgy for Ordinary Radicals* (Zondervan), 2010.